MAURITIUS
500 Early Postcards

The editor wishes to thank Sarah Dumez for her invaluable
assistance in making this book possible.

The image on page 268 is extracted from Denis Piat, *L'Île
Maurice, Sur la route des épices* (Paris: Les Éditions du
Pacifique, 2010), and reproduced with permission.

EDITORS: Fatia Guelmane, Julien Bourdry, Pierre Bernfeld
EDITOR (ENGLISH EDITION): James Lui
TRANSLATED FROM FRENCH BY: Lyn Parry
DESIGNER: Lisa Damanyanti
CURATOR OF THE COLLECTION: Marie Claude Millet
COLOUR SEPARATOR: SC Graphic, Singapore / PICA, Singapore

Published with assistance from

ISBN: 978-981-4260-47-3

Editions Didier Millet
121 Telok Ayer Street
#03-01
Singapore 068590
www.edmbooks.com

Printed in Singapore by Tien Wah Press (Pte) Ltd,
Singapore, October 2012.

MAURITIUS
500 Early Postcards

André de Kervern & Yvan Martial

EDITIONS DIDIER MILLET

CONTENTS

MESSAGERIES MARITIMES

MARSEILLE DJIBOUTI
AFRIQUE ORIENTALE
MADAGASCAR
LA REUNION MAURICE

FOREWORD

The postcard collection of André de Kervern offers us a unique and moving insight into the history of Mauritius. This collection tells the tale of Mauritian life at the dawn of the 20th century, and accurately captures the landscapes, the customs and the people of Mauritius before World War II – a Mauritius that was once home to British colonists, steam engines, vintage automobiles and an economy centred around sugar cane.

Through this collection, we can step back in time and recapture the splendour of the architectural heritage of old Mauritius. Better than any exhibition or history book, the postcards bring to life a Mauritius built to the rhythms of colonization and waves of immigration.

There remains little today of the Dutch colonial administration of the 17th century, and there is even less of the Portuguese navigators who are said to have discovered the island a century earlier. And of course the pirates who fled from the Caribbean and sought refuge on the island were careful not to leave any traces, preferring the island to be forgotten in case anyone might uncover their treasure on it.

It was not until 1735, when Governor Mahé de La Bourdonnais arrived on the island, that it began its transformation from shanty towns made up of a few scattered primitive huts. By the time of his departure 12 years later, Port Louis had been turned into a bustling port town, complete with its own shipyards, workshops, a Government House, neatly arranged streets and a fortress.

André de Kervern's postcards, however, do not date from this era, but instead show us what was left after the continual development and rebuilding of an island sitting at the crossroads of commerce and immigration from Europe, India, China and Africa. These postcard images stir up our emotions and awaken our curiosity. Each one tells a story, and together, they form a pictorial history of Mauritius, which local historians have yet to explore – there has yet to be a history of Mauritius in postcards. With more than 500 specimens, this book aims to fill this void.

ABOVE: A coastal road, lined with casuarina trees, leading to an estuary that stretches out to a barrier of volcanic basalt; Macondé can be viewed in the distance.

OPPOSITE: A poster advertising the destinations offered to the people of East Africa and the islands of southwestern Indian Ocean by the ships of Messageries Maritimes.

SOME BACKGROUND ON MAURITIAN POSTCARDS

Remote as it may seem in the middle of the Indian Ocean, Mauritius has not suffered from its geographical location. Instead it proved to be a great asset to the island in the 18th century, sitting on the western gateway to the shipping routes between the Old World and the New. Ships passing from faraway shores kept its people up-to-date with new developments, particularly from both north Atlantic coasts and the countries bordering the Indian Ocean. Despite being part of the French overseas empire that was embroiled in the Thirty Years' War, the War of Austrian Succession and the American War of Independence, Mauritius emerged largely unscathed. As it entered the 19th century, Port Louis remained a popular port of call for tall ships and the first steamships. Crews always had time to go ashore and, with a drink in hand, chat with the locals in the bars, regaling them with their experiences and discoveries in Paris, London, Boston, Oporto, and also in Bombay (Mumbai), Madras (Chennai), Canton (Guangzhou), Shanghai, Jakarta, Singapore and Kuala Lumpur.

British officials also established a presence. In 1810 the British arrived, having taken control during the Napoleonic Wars. Newly appointed to the island, their officials enjoyed talking about the technology that existed elsewhere but had not yet reached the shores of Mauritius, including the different ways of engraving and etching. The world of graphic reproduction became accessible to everyone with the application of these new illustration techniques. Art, once reserved only for the privileged or religious, reached the remotest of villages, and crossed the threshold of the most modest hut. In the 19th century, illustrations could be purchased from pedlars who travelled from village to village hawking their wares to the most humble households. This triggered the thirst for literacy, reading, knowledge and culture.

Religious art was still revered and admired. However, a hardened atheist probably would not have been converted by Michelangelo's *Pietà*, or the suffering of Christ painted by Rouault, whereas a devout believer would have fallen to his knees before an Agnus Dei of St Sulpice. It has to be remembered that in Mauritius, religious art is just as likely to be Hindu and Buddhist as it is to be Christian (or even Muslim, so long as it is calligraphic).

This was, however, not enough to spur the development of postcards in Mauritius. In the twilight years of his life, Father Jacques Désiré Laval, the Apostle of Mauritius, who was the first to be made a saint during the pontificate of Karol Wojtyla (John Paul II, 1979–2005), was worried that he would not live long enough to see the completion of the church of St Croix in the northern district of Port Louis. Funding

Until 1883, the image of Queen Victoria appeared on Mauritian postage stamps. This was followed by a series showing the Mauritian coat of arms. These were among the few postage stamps in the British Empire that did not show an image of a crowned sovereign. In 1899, England went one step further by issuing a postage stamp in honour of the French governor Mahé de La Bourdonnais on the bicentenary of his birth.

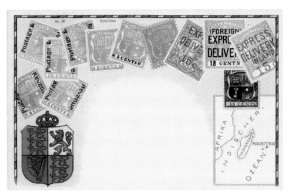

was of the utmost importance, and something had to be done urgently to raise money. By coincidence, Modeste Chambay, one of the earliest photographers in Mauritius, offered to take the priest's photograph. But the priest was too modest, and refused. However, when it was explained to him that the reproductions of his two photographs by Chambay and Lecorgne would be put up for sale, and the proceeds would provide the finances necessary to finish his beloved St Croix church, Father Laval forgot his misgivings, and posed for his photo. Father Laval died on 9 September 1864. These were perhaps the first illustrated postcards ever produced, even before Stéphan and Hermann introduced them into Austria in 1865 and 1869 respectively.

However, the fervour that Mauritians had for religious portraits was not the only explanation for the development of postcards on the island. The military and the engineering profession have long understood the value of drawings representing places and objects. One only needs to refer to Leonardo da Vinci's technical drawings to appreciate how an illustration is much more accurate than simply a verbal description.

Apart from soldiers and engineers, specialists such as architects, builders, navigators, cartographers and botanists also felt a pressing need to capture and study images and other graphical representations. The Mauritian archives carefully preserve a collection of all the plans, maps, impressions, panoramic views and topographic surveys of the island.

These illustrations were so well executed that they presented two aspects of their subjects: the horizontal and vertical (or bird's eye) views. Navigators, including pirates, would never set sail without a painter on board. He would

be called upon, for example, to reproduce the exact view of the entrance to the harbour at Port Louis from ten leagues away, five leagues, four, three, two and one. He might also be ordered to sketch the bloody scenes of a naval action. The artist who joined up as part of an expedition would have to sketch detailed and accurate illustrations of places, scenes, plants and animals, and also details such as seeds, buds, flowers and fruits. It is for this reason that the collection of lithographs by Jacques-Gérard Milbert make up a truly iconic album, although not photographic, of Mauritius in the early 19th century.

In the *Dictionnaire de biographie mauricienne*, Auguste Toussaint wrote that, based on the recommendation of the artist and member of the Institute of France, François-André Vincent, Milbert was appointed by Napoleon in 1800 to join Captain Nicolas Baudin's scientific expedition as draughtsman. When he landed on what was then still l'Île de France on 16 March 1801, he was too ill, like many other members of the same expedition, to continue the journey and he had to extend his stay until 16 December 1803.

Milbert used his recovery period to study and undertake research in collaboration with Lislet Geoffrey, Céré, Le Juge, and Thomi Pitot. He documented his findings in an album called *Voyage pittoresque à l'île-de-France, au cap de Bonne-Espérance et à l'île de Ténériffe*. It was

TOP: An engraving illustrating the construction of Port Louis under the direction of La Bourdonnais.

ABOVE: A print illustrating the occupations of the Dutch settlers in the 17th century.

TOP: The iconic dodo of Mauritius.

ABOVE: A postcard showing the dodo, painted by Georges Edwards as an illustration from his book *Gleanings of Natural History*, published from 1758 to 1764.

published in Paris in 1812 in two volumes and with an atlas containing a series of views of Mauritius. Auguste Toussaint considers this, along with *Voyage à l'île-de-France* by Bernardin de Saint-Pierre and the works of Bory de Saint-Vincent, as one of the best travel books on Mauritius at the time.

In the same vein was the artist Antoine Roussin. Although this talented painter owed his fame to his work on the island of Réunion and not Mauritius, his work here earned him renown as one of the major illustrators of the island before the age of photography.

The British were also represented – by Temple and Bradshaw. Temple was known for his prints of the British invasion of Mauritius in late November 1810, and the defeat of French troops under the command of Governor Charles Mathieu Isidore Decaen. He was also responsible for a series of prints on the advance of British troops along Chemin Vingt Pieds, Cape Malheureux, the camp at Moulin à Poudre, the skirmishes at the foot of Long Mountain and Terre Rouge, and the capture of Port Louis. Bradshaw, on the other hand, was a fine landscape painter, and the French painter, Thuillier, painted pleasant views of Port Louis during the first three decades of the 19th century.

There may well be sketches scattered throughout the island that travellers made during their visits to Mauritius in the middle of the 19th century. However, these graphic testimonials have yet to be comprehensively documented. When that is completed it will doubtlessly leave us with a true account of life in Mauritius at that time. The way of life changed completely over this period. Now that the endless Anglo-French wars were over, political, economic and administrative stability seemed here to stay. Île de France had become Mauritius, a British colony, but its population remained mainly French- or Creole- speaking, and Catholic. The slaves were emancipated and most of them turned their hands to skilled work such as building or carpentry, and avoiding at all costs working in the sugar cane fields, which only brought back dreadful memories of their enslavement. Their places in the sugar cane plantations were now taken by Indian agricultural labourers.

In just a few decades the population of Mauritius grew from 150,000 to 350,000, with three quarters of the population originating from India. This figure included both Hindus and Muslims. The former already accounted for 52 per cent of the population, and the latter around 17 per cent. Serious epidemics halted the growth of the population, keeping it at 450,000 until 1948, when malaria was eradicated by powerful doses of DDT. A rapid spurt in population growth followed, with demographic growth topping three per cent per year in the 1960s. This had dropped considerably by the 1970s thanks to government campaigns to use natural family planning methods (no pills or intra-uterine contraceptive devices), which were backed by the Catholic Church. Today population growth has stabilized at around 1.2 per cent per year. This however has sparked concerns about an ageing Mauritian population. One solution is to turn to the immigrant labour market. The textile, construction, public works and deep sea fishing sectors are increasingly hiring foreign workers from Bangladesh, Sri Lanka, China and Madagascar, arguing that it is necessary in order to fulfil their contracts, and keep up with orders. Owners of small sugar cane plantations also envisage bringing in cane cutters from overseas since the Mauritians themselves are less and less inclined to take up such work.

In the second half of the 19th century, Mauritius had achieved a stable economic and political environment, and certain parts of the community began to rise in status and wealth. The Franco-Mauritian oligarchy were the first to benefit from improving times, followed by the élite amongst coloured people, who were the offspring of inter-racial couples, married or unmarried. These couples were generally French colonists and slaves or cane cutters of African, Madagascan, Tamil or Indian origin. Later, wealthy Muslim, Tamil and Chinese traders came to the island to make their fortunes, thus creating an upwardly mobile society amongst those Mauritians of Indian or Chinese origins, of the Muslim, Hindi and Buddhist faiths. These successive gentrifications led to the adoption of middle-class values and attitudes that accompany expectations of a higher standard of living, and stimulate demand for greater cultural life.

The rising middle class commissioned talented painters to immortalize a favourite ancestor, a family home, an estate or even a more down-to-earth subject such as a horse or a sailing boat. The second half of the 19th century saw the emergence of accomplished Mauritian artists such as Alfred Richard, Alfred de La Hogue, Louis Sérandat de Belzim, Isis Boucherat, Henri le Sidaner, Xavier Le Juge de Segrais and Gabriel Gillet. A few of them, such as le Sidaner and Prosper d'Épinay, settled in Europe where they achieved fame and success. Portraits of prominent Mauritians from all backgrounds were almost always painted. It would indeed be a Herculean task to gather all these works of art, catalogue them and present them as a permanent exhibition. A museum may be unfeasible, and we might have to rely upon André Malraux's concept of the imaginary museum over half a century ago, but perhaps a virtual museum of our times – a computerized database – could be the answer.

By the second half of the 19th century, the first photographers were already making their appearance on the island. They came as simple travelling salesmen, laden with trunks containing the latest in silverware and fine porcelain, or sometimes offering dictionary or encyclopedia subscriptions in a market already dominated by Pierre Larousse. Others, more discreetly, arrived at Chien de Plomb, at the quay at Place Labourdonnais, with their cameras in large boxes and mounted on tripods, behind which the operator stooped covered by a piece of cloth so black that no light could get through.

As soon as they reached Mauritius's shores, the photographers raced to the office of the main newspapers at Port Louis, pleading with them to insert advertisements promoting their services in their papers, targeting locals who wanted to sit for portraits. Every pose, every photo, every framed portrait was a guarantee of further bookings, since word travelled fast on the island: "Who took that for you?" "How can I contact your photographer?" "Does he come to the house? I don't know when I'll get another chance like this!"

In fact, photographers were frequent visitors to the island. Port Louis was already well-connected with the rest of the world, thanks to several shipping companies which plied regular

Captain A. Mentys's vessel the *Dalblair*, wrecked on the reef at Pointe d'Esny during the cyclone of 5 February 1902.

TOP: The Chinese Banyan or *Ficus microcarpa*, a member of the fig tree family, is cultivated as an ornamental tree. It can grow to huge dimensions, both in height and girth. A native of Asia, it was introduced to Mauritius in the 17th century.

ABOVE: The Sockalingum Meenatchee Ammen temple on Nicolay Road is a major place of worship for Mauritians.

routes to ports such as Durban, the Cape of Good Hope, Aden, Galle, Bombay, Calcutta, Canton, Jakarta, Freemantle, Marseille, Southampton, Liverpool, Antwerp, Rotterdam, Oporto and Boston. Amongst these companies, the Mauritians preferred Messageries Maritimes, and the English companies Castle Lines, Clan Lines and P&O (Peninsular and Oriental Steam Navigation Company).

Most of the photographers were just passing through, but a few decided to stay on and settle permanently, contributing to the photographic heritage of the island. This was the case with Chambay, Lecorgne, Bonet and Drenning and his daughter. The story of the photographer Modest Chambay is worth recounting. Born on 10 October 1827 at Damigny in Normandy, Cambay was the son of a linen manufacturer and landed in Mauritius in August 1854. He arrived with another photographer, Alexandre Guillaume Louis Lecorgne. On 8 September 1854 the local newspaper *Le Cernéen* published a glowing article about them and their exhibition at rue de l'Eglise (Sir William Newton Street today). The following year they moved to Chaussée Street. In March 1860, Chambay and Lecorgne photographed the Apostle of Mauritius, Father Jacques Désiré Laval: one shot of him sitting, the other standing at the foot of a cross, in the style of Grünewald and his Isenheim Altarpiece. Chambay returned to France in 1860,

and submitted his photographs to *L'Illustration* magazine, which loved them. In December 1860 Chambay and Lecorgne became naturalized British citizens.

Chambay then returned to Mauritius in March 1861, bringing the latest photographic equipment. In 1864, he returned to France for good, while Lecorgne decided to stay longer on the island. We can trace Chambay's stay in Paris: in 1867, he opened his studio on 25 Avenue Montaigne, and took part in an exhibition organized by the French Society of Photography at the Palais de l'Industrie (the Grand Palais today). That same year he returned to Mauritius with another photographer, Bonet. On 8 December 1874 *Le Cernéen* praised their talents as portrait photographers. In 1875, Chambay went back to Paris again. Raymond d'Unienville, in the *Dictionnaire de biographie mauricienne*, recorded his death in around 1900.

The Mauritians, meanwhile, tired of foreign photographers calling all the shots, took things into their own hands. They learnt from these foreign photographers, asking questions about the equipment and accessories, and obtained their own. Local photographers included Gentil, Rambert, Déhaut, Vidal, Grégoire, Appavou, Béchard and the Halbwachs family. Mauritians of Chinese descent also joined the ranks with photographers such as François Lim, Lam Yee Chiu and Kwon Pak Hin.

The great popularity of postcards in late 19th- and early 20th-century Mauritius is due to several factors. The first is that Mauritians were travelling more during this time. Before 1850, the only people who travelled were those who left the island to settle elsewhere, for example in Europe, South Africa, Australia, India or China. However, there were other reasons to travel now, education being one of them. The colony had launched a grant scheme for overseas studies. Each year, the best students were awarded undergraduate scholarships for further studies abroad, along with return tickets by boat at the beginning and the end of their university courses.

Other opportunities to travel came from the improvement in working conditions and social status. The civil service recruited qualified students from the Royal College, first established at Port Louis, and later at Curepipe. When these Mauritian civil servants climbed high enough in the administrative hierarchy, they were awarded a paid vacation every six or seven years. This included a return ticket by boat for the employee and his family. Furthermore, the wealthiest families in the private sector – the sugar barons and those with successful businesses – could also afford to travel abroad. The most affluent of these families headed straight to Europe, a dream destination for them in the late 19th century. One of these members of the economic élite, Georges Thomy Thiéry (1823–1902), owner of a sugar plantation and a broker, decided to make a name for himself by becoming a patron of the Louvre and bequeathing to the museum his collection of paintings from the Barbizon school.

Those who had the opportunity to travel were almost always expected to describe what they saw to their countrymen when they returned home, and here was where postcards proved handy. Readily available wherever they went, the postcard served as a better memento of their travels to their loved ones back home than any travel memorabilia that could be found in a souvenir shop.

The third reason for the popularization of the postcard in Mauritius – as in anywhere else in the world – is that it is more down-to-earth. Letter writing is a time consuming task, and a strict set of formalities has to be respected. One cannot simply scribble a few words upon a blank sheet of paper, slip it into an envelope and drop it off at the post office. Such a slapdash way of letter writing could be taken as an insult. There was of course the telegram, but this was limited to short, clipped sentences. Also, the telegram is sometimes considered the bearer of bad news, and is opened with a trembling hand in anticipation of the worst.

There are no such problems with postcards. On the back, half the space is reserved for the address and the other half for the message, which must be short. It is the perfect solution for lazy letter writers, who want to keep in touch, yet would not want to spend too much time on the task. The postcard is informal. Just a few words will do, or one or two trivial sentences, a hello, a greeting, a signature, and the message is complete. The recipient, equally busy as the sender, will be glad to receive it, and will not be offended by the lack of long and cumbersome established forms of courtesy.

Presumably some foreign visitors in the last quarter of the 19th century were surprised at not being able to find postcards showing views

TOP: The carriages of Port Louis disappeared in the 1960s, due to the popularity of shared cabs.

ABOVE: Rochester Falls at Souillac. Like an organ, the falls augment the sound of water tumbling off the basalt cliff and turn it into music.

TOP: An artist's impression of the fancy dress ball given by the wife of Governor William Maynard Gomm (1842–1849) on 21 September 1847. To send out the invitations, Lady Gomm used, for the first time, the first postage stamps engraved and printed in Mauritius – the Post Office stamps.

ABOVE: The façade at the rear of Château du Réduit, the former residence of the governors of Mauritius, and the current one for the presidents of the Mauritian Republic.

OPPOSITE PAGE, ABOVE: Ancient straw huts in the suburbs of Port Louis.

OPPOSITE PAGE, BELOW: A view of the Corps de Garde and the hills of the St Pierre plains, as seen from Cascavelle and Casela.

of Mauritius. A local newspaper echoed their sentiments, and this was sufficient impetus to address the gap. There were two favourable conditions that helped. Experienced foreign photographers knew exactly which type of photographs were needed, and proceeded to take pictures of key buildings and monuments in Port Louis and other major towns, as well as landscape shots of the Pamplemousses garden, Pouce Mountain, the Pieter Both, the Lion and the Morne Brabant, and the Île Mouchoir Rouge and Mahébourg harbour.

They sent their pictures to established postcard manufacturers in Europe, and left the distribution and sales to locals in Mauritius and neighbouring islands. The Mauritians took to it quickly. Why leave to foreigners what they could possibly do better themselves, given their greater knowledge of local scenery and folklore? No sooner said than done: new photographs, this time taken by Mauritians themselves, replaced those taken by foreigners on millions of postcards later shipped to Mauritius. It is easy to spot the difference between Mauritian postcards and their foreign counterparts, firstly in terms of language. The captions for the Mauritian postcards were more likely to be written in French, whereas the foreign postcards were generally in English.

The incongruity of the captions also gives a clue to the origin of the postcard. Foreigners would generally label buildings and monuments in a different way from how locals did it. It was not possible to completely rule out mistakes by overseas producers, especially as they would not consult Mauritians on the accuracy of the captions. The following unique collection of postcards prior to the Second World War, compiled by André de Kervern, presents an incomparable variety of views of this island of 1,865 square kilometres, with a population of nearly 450,000.

The history of the postcard in Mauritius cannot be discussed without mentioning Allister Macmillan's book *Mauritius Illustrated*. Admittedly this is more of a photo album (excellently researched) of early 20th-century Mauritius than a collection of postcards, but this 450-page book containing 600 photographs is incontestably the best justice that we could do to Mauritius in the years prior to 1913 (when the book was published), a period known in France as the *Belle Époque*.

Initially, cameras were only available to professional and experienced photographers. They worked methodically and rigorously, and only photographed subjects which were worth capturing on film. Every photograph was carefully documented and archived, clearly indicating the location, the date and the photographer. These photographs took pride of place in the home, in the family photo album or hanging side by side with the portraits of parents and offspring.

As photography became more widespread, professional cameras in heavy boxes mounted on tripods gradually gave way to simple hand-held box cameras with an affordable price tag. Now anyone, not just professionals, could document their daily lives with simple snapshots. However, these photos when developed were, at best, placed in a photo album, often without captions, or in the worst scenario thrown into bundles and kept in a shoebox. Some information about the subject of this photograph, or its date, may be written on the back, but that is rare. Although such pictures immortalize a precious moment, they tend, over time, to be lost or discarded, which is a great pity. That is the reason why it is much easier to find pre-World War I pictures of Mauritius today, than those taken after World War II.

The history of Mauritian postcards is never final and no one would be more suited to keep it up-to-date than Tristan Bréville. A man who knows all there is to know about the subject, he has dedicated the last 40 years to assembling his marvellous collection of negatives, documents, photos, old post cards, cameras and photographic accessories. He and his wife Marie-Noëlle created and headed the Musée de la Photographie together, housed in a colonial building on the Rue du Vieux-Conseil in the centre of Port Louis. The collection includes photographs of the constantly changing heritage of the island.

Mauritius has undergone many changes from the 17ᵗʰ to the 21ˢᵗ centuries. First French, then British, the island has welcomed people from diverse origins, who have achieved more than simply living harmoniously together: they make up the Mauritian people. An independent republic since 1992, Mauritius is a multi-ethnic island – a melting pot of cultures, lifestyles, religions – which has forced the original élites to share power with emerging talents from India and China. Even though it is difficult to unravel this interwoven heritage, each Mauritian feels that he does play a part in the history of the island – a story of immigrants who have become brothers.

Environs de Port-Louis.
Vicinity of Port-Louis.
Cliché Gentil.

Audusson et Vidal — Mauritius

Usine de sucre de cannes

Sugar cane factory.

Charrette de cannes à sucre
* * * * *

Sugar cane harvest. The cut cane will be loaded onto carts pulled by oxen.

Huts in the middle of the sugar cane fields.

A crane unloading the sugar cane from carts and trucks.

NORTH

The northern region of Mauritius resembles an immense triangular plain, with its uppermost tip seemingly chopped off. Towards the south lies the Moka mountain chain, a barrier well nigh impassable. Only a few steep paths lead to the crest, allowing hikers to cross its peaks.

However, this mountain chain doesn't run from west to east, that is, from coast to coast. At its western edge, between the foot of the Montagne des Signaux and the coast, there is a mountain pass a little over one kilometre long, often swamped by vehicles. It is a constant scene of traffic congestion: indeed given how narrow the passage is, even the slightest accident, or break-down, will hold up the traffic flow. To the east of the Moka mountain range, a vast extension of the northern plain stretches to the coast. But the eastern and northern plains differ in their respective altitudes: whereas the eastern Flacq plains rise gradually from sea-level to around 500 metres over a distance of just 20 kilometres, the northern plains only reach an altitude of 250 metres.

The northern plains are covered with swathes of endless sugar cane fields. The monotony of the landscape is only broken by major villages, such as Goodlands, Triolet and Rivière du Rempart. In the north, where the temperatures are higher than the rest of the island, the inhabitants spend their days outdoors, which creates a particularly lively ambiance in the towns. At the foot of the Moka mountains the villages are situated in wooded valleys where the air is fresher, and blows cooler than on the plains.

The coastal towns, with their bustling open-air lifestyle, are very different from the inland villages. The residents of the inland towns, suffocating in their overheated houses, are tempted down to the coast by its refreshing sea breezes, beautiful coastal scenery and animated atmosphere. Everyone flops down under the shade provided by the rich foliage of the fig, Indian beech and casuarina trees. Both visitors and tourists should not be surprised when these sought-after spaces at the foot of a tree are suddenly transformed into fishmonger's stalls or dance floors, if they are not already being used as peddlar's pitches, construction sites, canoe repair shops, or even workshops for making fishing nets. The sheltered coves attract an increasing number of tourists, and the pretty sandy beaches and crystal clear waters are a haven for a growing number of swimmers, water-sport enthusiasts, sunbathers, picnickers, and toddlers building sand castles.

Literally ghost towns after severe malaria outbreaks from 1867 to 1948, the coastal villages have changed radically since the 1960s, and are thriving seaside resorts today. Their revival is due to the influx of wealthy Mauritians who escape the chilly temperatures of the higher altitudes and the Basses Plaines Wilhems in the winter months of July, August and September, by coming down to the coast to enjoy the warmer climate at private seaside bungalows. Before World War II, the government had offered low-cost leaseholds of beach fronts to affluent families, which spurred the growth of holiday bungalows and encouraged them to spend the winter season at the coast. This had the knock-on effect of creating much-needed seasonal jobs for the locals, such as cleaners, gardeners, guards or boatmen.

Today, demand far exceeds supply as an increasing number of people dream of becoming the proprietor of a plot of land with its own beach. These stunning

A. Appavou. 79. Mauritius. Suger Estate „Schoenfeld".

Schoenfeld sugar refineries were found close to the towns of Rivière du Rempart, Poudre d'Or, Hamlet and Espérance Trébuchet.

9 — Pamplemousses - Traveller's trees Alley

14 — Bassin du Jardin des Pamplemousses
Édition des Magasins Réunis
Reproduction interdite

TOP: Traveller's Palm (or Ravenela) Alley in the Pamplemousses Botanical Garden. In the foreground, there are some excellent examples of the palm tree.

ABOVE: The pond in the Garden, now populated by water lilies.

beachfront landscapes, even the most cramped, are snapped up as soon as they become available.

Before 1960, the population was largely seasonal holidaymakers, but a growing number of them have become full-time residents, converting their makeshift summer residences, with their flimsy ravenale walls and sugar cane leaf or vetiver roofs, into luxury homes with private swimming pools. These coastal villages have turned their backs on the uncivilized image that they once had, and are now competing with urban areas in terms of infrastructure and facilities. Electricity, running water, telephone lines, Internet access, satellite television and a decent road network are now all part of everyday life in these coastal towns. The opening of new restaurants, clubs, chic shops and supermarkets is the direct result of the expanding tourist sector.

Without doubt, the residents enjoy a privileged lifestyle with bright-blue landscapes and sun-soaked shores complemented by a vast array of water sports. The coastal population, once heavily reliant upon the visitors who came down from the highlands, has adapted easily to this new way of life; especially the young people, who benefit from the new job opportunities that this flourishing tourist industry creates. Tourists find contact with the colourful, cosmopolitan Mauritian people extremely enriching, and this cultural exchange opens up new horizons for the younger generation.

The young people, however, haven't completely turned their backs on their ancestry. In Mauritius the family unit and the values it represents are a strong reference point for children. It is of utmost importance to the Mauritius people, as well as to expatriates, that their roots are not forgotten.

The North is a tourist hub, welcoming around a million tourists every year. There is something for all tastes here, from visiting cultural and historical sites, trekking through lush tropical landscape, to soaking up the sun on one of the golden beaches. This region is full of charm with beautiful secluded islands, offering a backdrop of green mountains and basaltic ridges, surrounded by a turquoise ocean, the spectacular Pamplemousses Botanical Garden with its countless gazebos, and wooded valleys stretching to the foot of the Moka mountains, haunted by the romantic legend of Paul and Virginie, as well as the genuine hospitality and kindness of the Mauritian people that strikes visitors most.

No wonder, therefore, that tourists throng to Mauritius in ever-increasing numbers, enchanted by the spectacular scenery and warm-hearted people. Each visitor to the island returns home with fond memories.

PAMPLEMOUSSES. - Grand Kiosque. - Jardin Botanique

Odette 28 Janv. 1910.

A gazebo in the Pamplemousses Botanical Garden, thatched with vetiver, built on an islet in the middle of one of the ponds.

48   ILE-MAURICE — Kiosque - Jardin des Pamplemousses

Edition des Magasins Réunis
Reproduction interdite

Another view of the gazebo.

Devanture du jardin de Pomplemousses.

MAURICE — Jardin Botanique

27 — Un coin du Jardın des Pamplemousses.

Cliché G. Déliout - Noel Gr...

Maurice - Le Jardin de Pamplemousses.

Allée des Palmiers, Jardin des Pamplemousses.
The Palm trees Avenue, Pamplemousses Garden.

5 — Pamplemousses - View of the Royal Botanical Garden

1 – **Pamplemousses** - Lake in the Royal Botanical Garden

Etang du Jardin des Pamplemousses

Edition des Magasins Réunis
Reproduction interdite

Bassin des Gouramis – Jardin des Pamplemousses

With best wishes. Victor Brett

13 – **Pamplemousses** - Farquhar Basin

Vegetation flourishes at the Pamplemousses Botanical Garden, where visitors will find fan palms (whose leaves are used by locals to fan themselves and the flames of coal or wood-fired ovens), royal palm trees and lakes bordered by aquatic plants such as raffia. There are also a number of ponds: the water lily pond, the Gouramier pond (named after a freshwater fish) and the Farquhar Basin, named in honour of the first English governor, who brought about an *entente cordiale* between French former colonists and troops, and English officials.

ILE-MAURICE — Kiosque - Jardin des Pamplemousses

Pamplemousses - Le Grand Kiosque

Les Kiosques dans l'Ilôt — Jardins des Pamplemousses

Pamplemousses - Kiosque du Duc d'York

Pamplemousses - Avenue du Tombeau de Paul & Virginie

Île Maurice. - Pamplemousses - Allée et Tombeau de Paul et Virginie

PAMPLEMOUSSES. - Tombeau de Paul et Virginie

A. Appavou. 69. Mauritius. Scenery in Pamplemousses Gardens.

Gazebos of all sizes are scattered around the Pamplemousses Garden, such as that named in honour of the Duke of York, the future King George V, who visited Mauritius in August 1901. The Indian almond or *Terminalia catappa*, grown on the island, was a favourite with his wife, the future Queen Mary.

Monuments in the park include the white marble Liénard obelisk, and the colonial mansion Château Mon Plaisir.

The Paul and Virginie Alley leads to the tomb of these fictitious lovers from Bernadin de St Pierre's 1788 novel of the same name.

17 — Maurice - L'Observatoire

MAURITIUS POSTAGE REVENUE
2 CENTS

Cliché G. Déhaut - Noël Grégoire

The Meteorological Observatory at Moulin-à-Poudre was named in honour of Prince Alfred, Duke of Edinburgh, son of Queen Victoria, who laid its foundation stone on 30 May 1870.

36   Observatoire Royal Alfred (Pamplemousses)   Edition des Magasins Réunis
Reproduction interdite

Shortly before the independence of Mauritius on 12 March 1968, the headquarters of the national meteorological station were moved to Vacoas.

39. - Ile Maurice. - Le Château de Labourdonnais

Cliché E. Gentil Fils

Collection A. Béchard & Cie — Reproduction interdite

Situated next to the villages of Mapou and Forbach is the splendid 19th-century colonial Château de Labourdonnais, worth visiting both for its architecture and beautifully furnished interior.

8. PAMPLEMOUSSES — Fête Indienne c l'Établissement Beau Plan
Pamplemousses - Indian festival at " Beau Plan " settlement

A religious festival at the Beau Plan sugar refinery at Pamplemousses. Among the many guests, note the women in their best festival saris.

Église des Pamplemousses

The church of St Francis of Assisi, built in 1756, is the oldest place of worship on Mauritius.

Celebrating the religious festival of Yamsé, or Ghoon, at Beau Plan.

Celebrating the religious festival of Yamsé at Bon Air.

An Indian festival at Beau Plan, where the *calipas* (wrestlers) demonstrate their skills.

This postcard dates back to the earliest railway system on Mauritius. It shows here the most vertiginous section, stretching over the ravine of the Grande Rivière Nord-Ouest.

Grand River. - Railway bridge

In 1856, Dr Ulcoq submitted a report recommending the construction of a railroad, which would facilitate the transport of supplies and produce to and from the 262 sugar refineries on the island.

44 — ILE-MAURICE - Nouveau Pont de la Grande Rivière Nord-Ouest

Edition des Magasins Réunis
Reproduction interdite

The Longbridge report on the feasibility of a railroad sytem was accepted. In 1860, another expert, Hackshaw, supported the report's recommendations and work began on the first two lines – North and Central-South.

ILE MAURICE — Panorama

Crossing the Grande Rivière Nord-Ouest, this viaduct measures 260 metres long and 46 metres high.

Mauritius. Grand River. N W. Suspension Bridge.

Spanning the Grande Rivière Nord-Ouest, this suspension bridge was a feat of engineering. Before there were washing machines the *dhobee*, or laundryman, washed dirty clothes in the river, leaving them to dry on the river banks.

18 — Pont suspendu (Grande Rivière N. O.)

n des Magasins Réunis
Reproduction interdite

The Grande Rivière Nord-Ouest was a natural barrier to the expansion of Port Louis. In the beginning only temporary wooden bridges were built across the river during periods of drought.

Le pont suspendu de la Grande Rivière
Grand River suspension bridge

Cliché Gentil

The foundation stone of the suspension bridge, designed by English architect Lloyd, was laid on 9 January 1837.

Mauritius. Suspension bridge — Grand River.

The suspension bridge was replaced, in 1924, by a wider metallic structure, which was itself replaced by yet an even wider bridge.

Grand River N. W.

The governor La Bourdonnais was responsible for the construction of a magnificent aqueduct, bringing drinking water from the Grande Rivière Nord-Ouest to Port Louis.

31. MAURITIUS. La Tour Koenig — Koenig historical Tower, Grand River.

Édition J. Grancourt et Cie - Tous droits réservés.

Mystery surrounds this abandoned tower near the Grande Rivière Nord-Ouest. Construction of the tower by Henri Koenig began in about 1850, but it was left unfinished. According to local legend, it is haunted by the ghost of a workman who had a fatal accident at the site.

Ancien Phare de la Pointe aux Canonniers. (Port-Louis)

The inauguration of the lighthouses at Pointe aux Canonniers and on Île Plate took place on the same day, 1 December 1855. The one at Pointe aux Canonniers, no longer in service, stands within the compound of Le Canonnier Hotel.

35

4. Station de Quarantaine de la pointe aux Canonniers
Quarantine Station of Canoniers point

Cliché G. Rehaut

The quarantine station at Pointe aux Canonniers was built on the site of an ancient 19th-century fortress. Decommissioned, it became a holiday resort in the 1950s. In the 1970s Gilbert Trigano decided to convert the premises into the first Club Med resort on Mauritius.

Entrée de la Baie du Tombeau

Many believe that the Baie du Tombeau on the northwest of Mauritius takes its name from the wrecking of the *St Géran* in August 1744, and from the drowning of Virginie, the heroine of Bernardin de St Pierre's novel. However, the shipwreck took place off the coast of Poudre d'Or northeast of Mauritius. In reality the bay derived its name from the wrecking of the English ship *Benjamin* off the coast on 23 May 1697. The name translates to "Tomb Bay", since the captain, George Weldon, was buried on the shore. The white tombstone stands as a landmark to other ships seeking to enter the bay.

Le Pic de la Vierge - Montagne Longue

Long Mountain is part of the Moka mountain range. It starts near to the top of the Pieter Both and extends to Terre Rouge. From the summit, there is a panoramic view over the northern plains and islands: Coin de Mire, Île Plate, Îlot Gabriel, Île Ronde and Île aux Serpents. It was perhaps from this vantage point that Feillafé, in November 1810, first spotted the British fleet that would capture Mauritius from the French.

Collection Père Laval - Reproduction Interdite - Cliché R. Haibwachs

ILE MAURICE. - Vue de Sainte-Croix - La Chaîne du Pieter Both

The postcard is entitled "Moka mountain range, view of St Croix". But it would be more precise if it read "View of Long Mountain", since we can see more of the eastern end, including the Pieter Both, whereas a view of St Croix should extend further to the west, showing notably Le Pouce and Montagne des Signaux.

37

Vue de la Plage de Mon Choisy. (Port-Louis)

The popular beach at Mont Choisy takes its name from Armand Jules de Montchoisy, captain of the Provence regiment who defended the island during the War of the Austrian Succession. Behind the backdrop of casuarina trees extends a plain that was used as a runway before World War II, and later as a football pitch.

Trou aux Biches — Pagode Hindoue

The Maheswarnath temple at Triolet is the starting point for a major annual pilgrimage, which ends at Grand Bassin. The pilgrimage takes place during the religious Maha Shivaratri festival, or the Great Night of Shiva.

Trou aux Biches — Les Pêcheries

Wealthy European families preferred the coastal resort of Grand Baie, whereas the affluent coloured families from Beau Bassin/Rose Hill, encouraged by the Mauritian government, flocked to the coastal town of Trou aux Biches.

A. Appavou. 17. Port Louis. Vallée des Prêtres.

Since the French colonization of the island in the 18th century, colonists who wanted to settle in Mauritius were offered special concessions. These privileges were extended to the Catholic parishes as well, such as St Louis, which was allotted the valley running along the foot of Long Mountain, hence its name Vallée des Prêtres, or the Valley of Priests.

Vallée des Prêtres.   Cliché Gentil.

The parish of St Louis had neither the financial nor human resources to exploit Vallée des Prêtres, and it remained proprietor in title only. Later, further legal problems resulted from the confiscation of church property during the French Revolution. The conflict between church and state continued over the period of British colonization (1810–1968). After the devastation of Cyclone Carol in February 1960, the church made a symbolic gesture and gave up its ownership rights over Vallée des Prêtres. The state then built homes in the valley for victims of the cyclone, and this new city was called "Cité La Cure".

PORT LOUIS

It is becoming more and more difficult to catch a glimpse of the Port Louis of postcards from the Belle Époque, in the period from the late 19th century to World War I. The 21st-century Port Louis is a bustling city with an ever-increasing number of high-rise ultra-modern buildings that attest to thriving commercial and financial activities. Today this city is more focused on its future, and its past is lost under swathes of modernity. Early postcards can help the visitor forget, for an instant, the hectic city with its traffic-congested streets, and take them back to a Port Louis that was built over two and a half centuries ago. Let's step back in time to discover what Port Louis was like before the arrival of the first Dutch and French settlers. The extensive views of the city from the Marie-Reine-de-la-Paix esplanade, or Fort Adelaide sweeping over the tops of the giant skyscrapers to the Moka mountains, make us forget momentarily the commercial hub of the city. Cradling Port Louis bay, this mountain chain, with its lush valleys and rugged crests, soars over the sea. Burbling creeks (Pouce, Créoles, Pucelles and La Paix), and the river Lataniers cut paths through the deep valleys, finally flowing out into the harbour, hollowing out a deep channel, pushing back the coral reef to beyond Tonneliers Island (Fort George) and Barkley Island (Fort William).

Tonneliers or Cooper Island was reclaimed from the sea by the building of an artificial causeway, which now links it to Port Louis. Initially, in the 1970s, this piece of land was marked out for a manufacturing free trade zone. However, the government changed its plans, and decided that the whole of Mauritius was to become a free trade zone. Now, the reclaimed land, known as Mer Rouge (the Red Sea) serves as a modern container and warehouse terminal for the constantly growing activities of unloading and processing raw marine produce, such

as tuna. Over the centuries the creeks and rivers have carved their way through the soils of Port Louis, hollowing out basins, such as that found at the East India Company Garden, or channelling around basaltic masses, such as the area around Government House, or the land sandwiched between the Pouce and Créole creeks, upon which Rempart and St Georges streets, and the barracks, stand. The construction of the railway, from 1862 to 1865, changed the seafront considerably, which was filled in and then raised to the same level as the Place du Quai and Grenier promontory. The Mauritius Dock warehouses (now the Caudan Waterfront complex) were also built on land reclaimed from the sea.

In Port Louis, land was reclaimed by draining the marshlands. These wetlands were formed on the floodplains that bordered the many rivers flowing down from the Moka valleys. Due to deforestation during the 19th century, the mountainsides are less densely wooded than they were when Mauritius was under the French, and the rivers flow less forcefully. However, it only takes a few hours of heavy tropical showers for these rivers to burst their banks in places, especially in the East India Company Garden. Port Louis occupies a low-lying basin, and it only needs heavy rains to coincide with high tides for Mother Nature to claim back what is rightfully hers, much to the dismay of residents and road

A. Apparoo.   57.   View of the Town of Port Louis & Harbour.

Ile MAURICE.—   1. - Port-Louis - Panorama (1)

TOP: A view of Port Louis looking out towards the harbour where sailing ships and steamships are anchored.

ABOVE: A panorama of Port Louis from the city centre to the west. In the left foreground are St Louis Cathedral (pre-1933) and the Bishop's Palace (1854). In the left background, Signal Mountain towers over the town.

Tranquebar, Port-Louis.   Cliché Gentil.

Fort Adelaide, Port-Louis   Cliché Gentil.

TOP: The hills of Tranquebar, formerly a rural suburb of Port Louis. Agricultural workers from the sugar plantations settled here in the early 20th century. These new city dwellers still clung to their rural origins – living in straw-roofed huts, keeping stables and growing vegetables.

ABOVE: Perched on Little Mountain, Fort Adelaide was built by the British around 1840, between the city centre and the Muslim district of Plaine Verte.

users. Fortunately this only happens once or twice every decade. In the early 18th century, the French governor Bertrand François Mahé de La Bourdonnais made some important urban improvements to the town. The central promontory was set aside for administration and public buildings. On the east side of town, the Champ de Mars was built in an ancient volcanic crater. The west side was reserved for the St Louis Cathedral, the parsonage, the courts, the Supreme Court, a police station, registration offices, Government House and the Place d'Armes (a military training ground for manoeuvres) surrounded by lodges, offices, warehouses and workshops.

A defensive wall closed off this administrative district, with lookout windows directly over the harbour, East India Company Garden and the barracks on the left, and over Royal Street and Pamplemousses Street on the right. At the bottom of the Place d'Armes the administrative promontory veers off to the right towards the harbour. Here stand the customs house, a windmill, the military and civilian hospitals, a barracks (Arabian dock), a boating pond (now the main market), the Parc à Boulets (Immigration Square), Trou Fanfaron Bay and an arsenal. The estuary of Pouce Creek formed a vast marshland (from the Treasury Office to Edith Cavell Street) on its floodplain which could only be crossed by jumping from stone to stone (the site of the East India Company Garden today). From 1778 to 1779, the engineer Chevalier de Tromelin built a causeway from Rempart Street (Edith Cavell Street)

to the Lodge of Government House, which allowed the inhabitants to cross over this former marshland on foot. The marshland eventually became filled in with silt deposited by the rivers whose passage to the open sea was blocked off by Tromelin's causeway. The channel still needs to be dredged frequently. Tromelin built another causeway linking Trou Fanfaron (today's Albion Dock) to Tonneliers Island, simplifying the access from Port Louis to the island, upon which stands Fort George, a La Bourdonnais military fortification. On the opposite side of the channel sits Fort Blanc (Fort William), known as the Batterie Royale prior to 1740, which was equipped with 35 cannon to protect Port Louis against attacks from the sea. Tromelin would have completed his consolidation plan of the harbour with a third causeway between Government House and Trou Fanfaron. Only archaeological excavations would be able to confirm this – and these are unlikely to happen in the near future.

The fire of 25 September 1816 destroyed virtually all the administrative buildings between the Place d'Armes and the Parc à Boulets. In their place rose the Port Louis of the British era (1810–1968). During this period several significant events took place, such as the emancipation of slaves (1835), the influx of Indian indentured workers (1834–1924), the municipalisation of the capital (1850), the development of the railroad system (1864–1865) and the devastating epidemics (1867–1948) which depopulated Port Louis, with people fleeing the city to settle in the towns of Plaines Wilhems (Beau Bassin, Rose Hill, Quatre Bornes, Vacoas, Phoenix, Curepipe) and the urban outskirts of Moka and St Pierre. In the 1960s, the first multi-storey buildings, such as the Anglo-Mauritus Building, began to make their appearance, as modern Port Louis emerged. In the pages that follow, thanks to André de Kervern's collection of post cards, the town of Port Louis is recaptured as it existed during its time under the British.

Port-Louis à vol d'oiseau.
Bird's eye view of Port-Louis.

Cliché Gentil.

Two bird's-eye views of Port Louis taken from Signal Mountain, spanning from the west to the centre of the city. The large square at the bottom right is the site of the central barracks. In the distance on the right, one can easily distinguish Tonneliers Island (Fort George) and the sand bank connecting it to the estuary of Terre Rouge River, which flows through the Roche Bois district. In winter the estuary is home to migratory birds, some from as far away as Siberia.

PORT-LOUIS. - Vue de la Citadelle

E. Vidal - Reproduction interdite

Panoramic view of Port Louis showing, from left to right,
Signal Mountain (extreme left), St Louis Cathedral, the
mid-19th century Bishop's Palace, Port Louis harbour,
Tonneliers Island in the distance, Fort George and Chaussée
Tromelin at bottom right.

PORT-LOUIS. - Vue de la Citadelle

la montagne du Pouce

12/7/05.

6 — **Port-Louis** – Statue de La Bourdonnais

L'écrivain se rappelle au bon souvenir de Monsieur Dollfus et lui envoie ses meilleures amitiés.

The statue of La Bourdonnais stands on the Place du Quai at Port Louis harbour.

62. **Mauritius.** Port Louis. Statue of Labourdonnais.

Governor Farquhar was the first to come up with the idea of erecting a statue in honour of La Bourdonnais. *Le Cernéen* – the newspaper started by Adrien d'Épinay – had complained that in 1832 there was still no statue commemorating the founder of Port Louis and Mauritius. Hence, on 30 August 1859, the first public statue in Mauritius, by French sculptor Dumon, was unveiled. In 1989, a replica of this statue was presented to the town of St Malo, the birthplace of La Bourdonnais.

7. MAURITIUS Labourdonnais Square and Place d'Armes. Port-Louis.

Édition J. Grancourt et Cie - Tous droits réservés

Two views of the statue of Bertrand François Mahé de La Bourdonnais. Born on 11 February 1699 at St Malo, he joined the merchant navy as a ship's boy and in 1718 entered the service of the French East India Company as a lieutenant. It was in 1723, while he was sailing in the Indian Ocean that he first arrived at Mauritius. At 34 he persuaded the East India Company to establish a French naval base in Mauritius, since the island was ideally situated at the northwest gateway to the ocean. He was to be the governor of Mauritius from 1735 to 1747. After the War of Austrian Succession he was appointed head of a fleet in Indian waters, which under his command won many brilliant victories against the English. But after a quarrel with Dupleix, he was recalled to France, where he lived a meagre existence until his death in Paris on 10 November 1753.

Mauritius

Port-Louis Harbour from Government House
Le Port, vu du Palais du Gouvernement

Place du Quai à Port Louis.

Four sketches of Port Louis. The artist captured this angle at the corner of Farquhar Road and the Place d'Armes. It shows, from left to right, the statue of La Bourdonnais, the Mauritius Dock warehouses, the headquarters of Blyth Brothers, a train passing through and a sailboat anchored in the waters of Chien de Plomb.

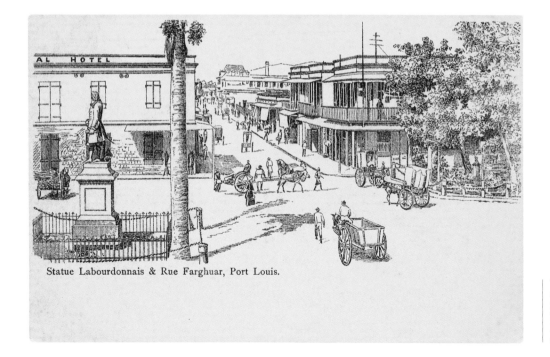

Statue Labourdonnais & Rue Farghuar, Port Louis.

The view here has been drawn from the corner of the Place d'Armes and Moka Road (renamed John Kennedy Street today). From left to right, you can see part of the Money Changers buildings (then a hotel), and Farquhar Road lined with shops.

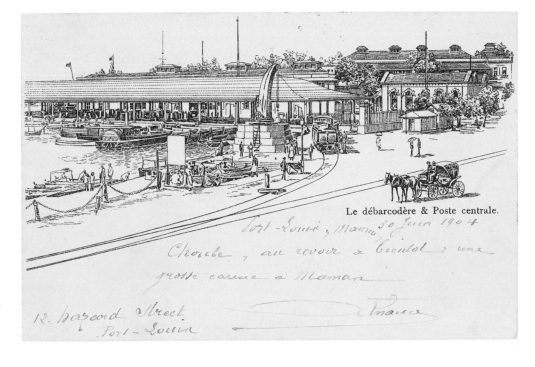

Le débarcodère & Poste centrale.

Port-Louis, Maurice 30 Juin 1904
Choube, au revoir à bientôt, une grosse caresse à Maman

12. Jasard Street Port-Louis

Further to the left of the previous site, this drawing shows the Chien de Plomb quay with its characteristic crane and the Customs warehouses in the background (today the Astrolabe waterfront shopping centre). At the far right sits the main post office.

"Few builders could have done as well [as him] in such a short time and with such limited resources," says historian Auguste Toussaint on La Bourdonnais. When he landed, Mauritius was inhabited by a handful of runaway slaves and swarms of rats. By the time he left he had founded a bustling port-city, the capital of a country, a naval base with a thriving shipyard and workshops, an arsenal, flourishing trades and an agricultural sector. Mauritius was now powerful enough to take on the British. The East India Company directors in Paris, unwilling to invest vast amounts of money in the colony, watched with astonishment as their own businesses declined while his thrived. His reply was, "I manage your affairs according to your instructions, and mine according to my own intuition." His successes earned him many enemies, and a stint in the Bastille, before he was finally exonerated of all accusations and freed from prison.

BI-CENTENAIRE

1735

1935

DE PORT-LOUIS

28. MAURITIUS. Rade de Port-Louis, du — Port-Louis Harbour from Goverment
"Gouvernement". House.

Édition J. Grancourt et Cie - Tous droits réservés.

La Bourdonnais' achievements were not confined to Mauritius. They extended to the rest of the Indian Ocean, and in particular, to the French naval and military challenge to British domination in the East Indies.

MAURICE — Square Labourdonnais

The statue of the famous Malouin by French sculptor Augustin Dumont, sponsored by public subscription and support from Governor Stevenson, was unveiled in 1859.

The success of La Bourdonnais earned him the envy of his peers, the distrust of his superiors and imprisonment in the Bastille.

In 1935, Mauritians celebrated the bicentenary of the founding of Port Louis by La Bourdonnais. This triumphal arch was erected in his honour at the Place du Quai.

A. Appavou. 25. Port Louis. Trou Fanfaron.

A view of Trou Fanfaron, one of the natural bays in Port Louis harbour. From 1834 to 1920, around 500,000 Indians landed here to work on the sugar plantations. In the 18th century tens of thousands of Tamils, Pondicherrians, Malays, Chinese, Africans and Madagascans disembarked at exactly the same place.

PORT-LOUIS. - Arrivée des Membres de la Commission royale - 18 Juin 1909

On 18 June 1909, royal commissioners Sir Franck A. Swettenham, Sir E. Loughlin O'Malley and H.B. Drysdale Woodcock arrived, on the sloop-of-war *Forte*, to study the economy of Mauritius and its sugar industry. This worried the elite and the affluent, who feared that the inquiry would bring about social recommendations in favour of the workers. Even before their arrival, the Mauritians were divided into supporters and opponents of this Commission of Inquiry. The commissioners eventually left the island on 24 August, and their recommendations were acceptable to all parties.

ILE-MAURICE — Ruisseau du Pouce à Port-Louis

Edition des Magasins Réunis
Reproduction interdite

The Pouce flows through the capital from the southeast to the northwest, finally reaching the sea at Port Louis harbour. After only a few hours of heavy rain on the peaks of the Moka mountain chain, this deceptively slim creek becomes a raging torrent, sometimes reaching the top of its retaining walls.

Forges et Fonderies Tardieu rue Bourbon (Port-Louis)

Edition des Magasins Réunis
Reproduction interdite

The Tardieu – or Colonial – forges and foundries on Bourbon Street, Port Louis, occupied an entire district. Before 1913, they stood on Nicolay Road, where there were already British forges and foundries. In contrast, the Tardieu forges were run by Mauritians (Esnouf, Régnard, Paturau, Leclézio). The British had another forge at St Pierre, while the Mauritians had one at Rose Belle.

Pleasure Garden Cassis

It was the idea of Aldor Rohan, one of the mayors of Port Louis, to create a "pleasure ground" or "flower garden" to provide residents with a place to stroll along the waterfront, with a view overlooking Port Louis harbour.

PORT-LOUIS. - Pleasure garden

Another mayor of Port Louis, Eugène Laurent, had hoped to build a sanitorium for people suffering from malaria, which ravaged Mauritius from 1867 to 1948, but it never materialized.

A. Appavou.   63. Mauritius.   Pleasure Gardens at Cassis.

For the inauguration of this magnificent flower-filled garden on 23 and 24 December 1905, there were fireworks, picnics, cakes, pirogue regattas and cycling races.

Le "Pleasure Ground„ - Port-Louis
The "Pleasure Ground", Port-Louis.   Cliché Gentil.

Up until 1905, Pleasure Ground was just a vast piece of wasteland between the harbour, the cemetery in the west and Fort William. In the late 19th century, a gas factory was built here to provide lighting for the streets of Port Louis. Decommissioned, the building is now a badminton court.

Un Kiosque au "Pleasure Ground,, - Port-Louis.
A Kiosk in the "Pleasure Ground", Port-Louis.

Cliché Gentil.

The layout of the new Pleasure Ground gardens led to the removal of Filao Alley, which, according to local musical folklore, was the haunt of Pierre Mangallon and his fellow stonemasons.

La chaussée, Port-Louis

Cliché Gentil.

After the devastating fires of 22 and 23 July 1893, and again those of 26 August 1896, Ivanov Manuel decided to build this beautiful Elias Mallac building (today the Harel Mallac). It was highly criticized during its time, as it seemed too modern and was discordant with the traditional wooden houses of old Port Louis.

Port-Louis.   Cliché Gentil.

A bridge in Port Louis spanning one of the creeks. In the distance lies the Moka mountain range, where one can just about make out Pieter Both.

Ruisseau du Pouce, Port-Louis.
Pouce Stream, Port-Louis.   Cliché Gentil.

Another bridge allows commuters on Desroches Road a crossing over Pouce Creek. Le Pouce, after which the creek is named, dominates the scenery.

PORT-LOUIS. - Boulevard Edouard-VII

58

At the beginning of the 20th century, Edward VII Boulevard was a favourite place for residents to take a stroll. The air was healthier and less dusty here than in the city centre.

PORT-LOUIS. - Boulevard Edouard-VII

59

Port-Louis

Courses au Champ de Mars

LE CHAMP DE MARS, PORT-LOUIS

PORT-LOUIS. - Les Courses

E. Vidal - Reproduction interdite

Port-Louis - Indiens au Champ de Mars

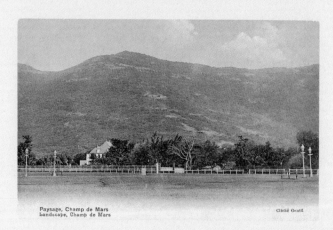

Paysage, Champ de Mars
Landscape, Champ de Mars

Cliché Gentil

Port Louis. Malartie tomb - Champ de Mars.

With the Compliments of the Season

20

Le Tombeau Malartic, Le Labyrinthe Laurent, la Montagne du Pouce.
Malartic Tomb, Labyrinth Laurent and the "Pouce" Mountain.
Cliché Gentil.

6. Jet d'eau du Champ de Mars et Tombeau Malartic
Fountain of the "Field of Mars" and Mallard Tomb

Cliché G. Rehaut

54   ILE-MAURICE — La Statue du Roi Edouard VII - Champ de Mars à Port-Louis

61

OPPOSITE PAGE:

The horse races at the Mauritius Turf Club (established in 1812), Champ de Mars, draw crowds of race-goers, punters and spectators, especially between April and December. The stands are reserved for the middle class, the Blagueurs de la Montagne tent for the punters, and everyone else crowds together in the "plain" – the rest of the open ground inside the racecourse. The first stands (centre left) were rudimentary, yet permanent, unlike the temporary boxes which were erected only for winter. The racecourse owed its initial popularity to Colonel Alfred Alured Draper who believed that horse-racing was a way to bring together the multi-ethnic communities of Mauritius. The racecourse's new stands (centre right) were built using reinforced concrete. Around 400 thoroughbreds compete during each racing season.

THIS PAGE:

(TOP LEFT AND RIGHT) Malartic's Tomb, an obelisk dedicated to Anne-Joseph Hippolyte de Maurès, Count of Malartic and penultimate French governor of Mauritius (18 June 1792–26 July 1800). Erected on the Champs de Mars, half of it was broken off by the cyclone of 29 April 1892.

(ABOVE LEFT) The charming Champ de Mars esplanade, before the statue of Edward VII was erected.

(ABOVE RIGHT) The statue of King Edward VII, by Mauritian sculptor Prosper d'Épinay, stands on an esplanade in the middle of the Champ de Mars racecourse.

Pari-Mutuel. Champ de Mars. (Port-Louis)

The Champ de Mars pavilion, amongst the stands of the Mauritius Turf Club in Port Louis, was used by gamblers. Its architecture was reminiscent of the best English and French racecourses. It was demolished in 1985.

La montagne des signaux, Le nouveau mât.
Top of Signal Mountain, Port-Louis

Cliché Gentil.

A new signal mast being erected atop Signal Mountain. Today, the mountain continues to play an important role in long-range communications, with the out-dated system of banners and flags replaced by sophisticated antennae receiving satellite signals.

Bathurst Creek, whose name was also given to a pipeline system, provided running water for the northern and eastern suburbs of Port Louis. It took its name from Lord Bathurst, Minister of the Colonies (1812–1827).

A Mauritius hemp factory on the banks of the Grande Rivière Nord-Ouest. In the right foreground are the ruins of a flour mill built in the time of French colonial rule.

L'entrée des Casernes du Port-Louis

Entrance of the Barracks Port-Louis

Cliché G. Rehaut

The northeastern entrance of Central Barracks, with its double-storeyed tower, opens out onto the city centre. The barracks, dating from the mid-18th century, was used as military headquarters until 1922, when it became the headquarters for the police force. A causeway, built by Tromelin, links Government House to the barracks.

5 — Hôpital Civil (Port-Louis)

Edition des Magasins Réunis
Reproduction interdite

Mauritius, situated at the southwest entrance to the Indian Ocean, was a main port of call for passing ships. This in turn created the need for a hospital to treat sick crew members. Governor La Bourdonnais was responsible for the construction of the first military and civilian hospital in the port. An infestation of plague-infected rats in May 1899 meant that the hospital had to be transferred to the premises of the Royal College on Madame Road (Volcy Pougnet Street today), whilst the college was relocated to Curepipe.

The College of the Christian Brothers on Government Road is today the Saint Jean Baptiste de La Salle school on Pope Hennessy Street.

Le Collège des Frères, Port-Louis
The College of the Christian Brothers

Cliché Geutil

II. - PORT LOUIS (Ile Maurice). - Le Collège St-Jean-Baptiste de la Salle

The Saint Jean Baptiste de La Salle school in Port Louis closed down due to chronic malaria outbreaks, and the brothers set up another school in Curepipe in 1877. They converted their Port Louis premises into a primary school open to children from all cultural and religious backgrounds.

Collection A. Béchard & Cie — Reproduction interdite

Port-Louis - Institut

On 25 October 1877 a devastating fire razed to the ground several buildings, amongst them the Universe Hotel. Today the Mauritius Institute stands in the same spot. On 20 July 1880, London gave its consent to build a museum and national library here.

PORT-LOUIS. - Le Musée

The foundation stone of the museum of Port Louis was laid on 27 November 1880. Since its opening, it has played host to many scientific, historic and cultural exhibitions. The National Library, founded in 1900, inherited an immense book collection from Sir Virgile Naz upon his death on 3 August 1901. The Institute opened to the public on 6 April 1903. On 4 December 1921, the patron of the arts Edgar de Rochecouste donated his collection of 40 paintings, including some Impressionist masterpieces, to the Institute.

22. MAURITIUS Le Musée. Port-Louis. — Port-Louis Museum.

Édition J. Grancourt et Cie - Tous droits réservés.

On 3 March 1939, the governor permitted the Mauritius Institute (Natural History Museum of Port Louis) to accept the shell collection bequeathed by Georges Antelme.

Port-Louis — La Douane

The ship in the foreground of this postcard would probably have plied the shipping lanes between the islands, long before regular airline connections. Behind is the former customs building where passengers were greeted as they stepped ashore from the boats.

La Poste Centrale (Port-Louis)

Edition des Magasins Réunis
Reproduction interdite

Situated in the port area, the Central Post Office handled post arriving overland by road and rail, as well as overseas mail delivered by boat or plane. This building, completed in 1868, started operations as the Central Post Office on 21 December 1870.

65. - PORT-LOUIS. - Poste Centrale

E. Vidal - Reproduction interdite

The Mauritian Central Post Office is well known amongst stamp collectors around the world. It was responsible for issuing limited editions of the first two postage stamps engraved and printed in Mauritius. The Post Office is still well remembered today, as it issues no more than 20 stamps each year, whose illustrations and themes are based on local heritage.

31 — Palais de Justice à Port-Louis

Edition des Magasins Réunis
Reproduction interdite

A view of the Palais de Justice or Supreme Court, Port Louis. On 14 August 1777, Jean-Baptiste Étienne Delaleu introduced the Code Delaleu, a compilation of laws still in force in Mauritius. Under the First French Empire, it was complemented by the Code Napoleon. This French system of laws remained in force even after the British captured the island in December 1810. Mauritian law is thus characterized by these two traditions, combining elements from the Napoleonic Code and the British legal system.

62. - PORT-LOUIS. - Cour suprême

E. Vidal - Reproduction interdite

French law (both the Delaleu and Napoleonic codes) became progressively anglicised under pressure from British judges, magistrates and officials. From 15 July 1847 onwards, Mauritian lawyers were required to plead in English. Meanwhile, witnesses and defendants could still address the judges and magistrates in French, or in a language commonly used, such as Mauritian Creole.

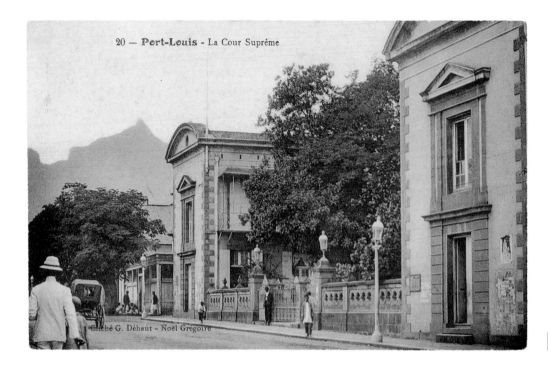

20 — Port-Louis - La Cour Suprême

Cliché G. Déhaut - Noël Grégoire

Another view of the Supreme Court building, which was completed in October 1851.

MAURICE -- Palais du Gouvernement

Government House on the Place d'Armes, Port Louis.

Port-Louis - Hôtel du Gouvernement

On 22 March 1742, the engineer Jacques de Belval drew up plans for La Bourdonnais Lodge, which included Government House. That same year, the engineer Antoine Marie Desforges-Boucher rebuilt Government House, which had been partially damaged by fire on 28 September 1737. On 1 October 1807, Jean Guérandel and Pierre Clément Texier started building the second storey. In 1816, Sergeant James Hastie saved Government House from a second fire.

61. - PORT-LOUIS. - Hôtel du Gouvernement

F. Vidal. Reproduction interdite

On 13 October 1832, Governor Colville suggested that the ground floor and the outbuildings of Government House be used for administrative offices. In the 1970s the outbuildings were demolished to make way for the New Government Centre complex and Vaghjee Hall.

On 20 April 1902, the government received a second statue of the late Queen Victoria. It was installed at the entrance to Government House, while the first statue stood before the Central Railway Station.

On 17 October 1848, a group of prominent Mauritians petitioned the British colonial government to establish a municipal council for Port Louis. The request was relayed to London, and Governor George William Anderson was charged with the task. On 31 August 1866, the newly founded city council took over the premises of Hôtel d'Europe and converted it into the town hall of Port Louis.

Louis - L'Hôtel de Ville

Cliché G. Déhaut - Noël Grégoire

During the French Revolution, there was already a municipal administration in Port Louis. On 29 June 1790, the French governor Conway offered the use of Government House as a town hall. This first municipal government was later abolished by the Napoleonic government under Governor Decaen.

Port-Louis - Hôtel de Ville

Another view of the town hall at Port Louis.

25. MAURITIUS Gare Centrale du Chemin de fer — Railway Central Station. Port-Louis.

Édition J. Grançourt et Cie - Tous droits réservés.

A view of Victoria Central Railway Station. On 10 July 1858, the engineer J. Longridge and his colleagues Stanley and Burnett arrived at Port Louis to start work on the new Mauritian railway. The inauguration of the North line took place on 23 May 1864. Work on the second line began on 26 June 1865. The first train ran from Port Louis to Mahébourg on 22 October. On 11 April 1871 the Savanais asked for an extension of the line between Rose Belle and Souillac, and this was sanctioned on 5 October 1875. The inauguration of this section took place on 11 December of the same year.

PORT-LOUIS. - La Gare

E. Vidal. Reproduction interdite

On 1 April 1879, the Mokassiens and Flacquois also had a railway line built from Rose Hill to the Grande Rivière Sud-Est. Work on the railway system ceased exactly one hundred years after its introduction. By then rail had been replaced by bus services, which were faster.

Port-Louis - La Gare Centrale

On 21 May 1897 a statue of Queen Victoria was delivered to the central railway station at Port Louis. Its inauguration took place on 22 June. Today this statue stands in the cellars of the Mahébourg Naval Museum.

RÉUNION

The Réunion pavilion housed the 1935 inter-island colonial exhibition, organized as part of the bicentennial celebrations of the town of Port Louis.

The Municipal Theatre of Port Louis during the Bastille Day celebrations of 1905. The first British governor, Robert Townsend Farquhar, laid its foundation stone. It was designed by architect Pierre Poujade and its interior decorated by painter Thuillier. It opened on 11 June 1822 and was presented to the colony of Mauritius on 3 August 1831.

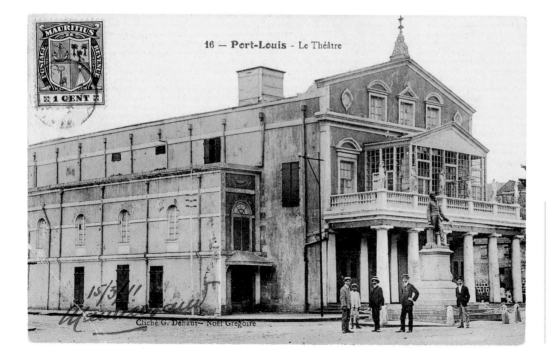

Drama wasn't always confined to the stage. British and French officers sometimes caused a scene as they settled their differences in the pit, or even in the boxes. Members of the audience occasionally voiced their protests against the British colonial and municipal authorities. The police complicated a situation already sensationalized by the tabloid press. On 5 September 1859, for example, the mayor, Pierre Nalzir Charron, had to give the order to use fire hoses to disperse trouble-making spectators from the theatre.

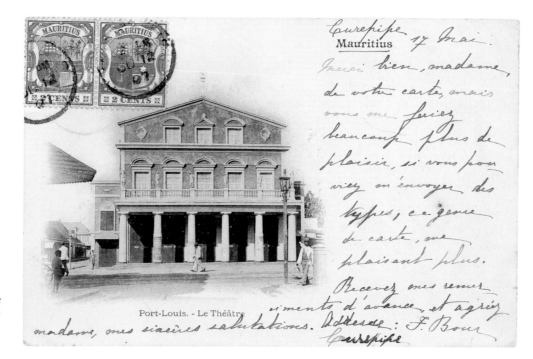

Mauritius

Curepipe 17 Mai.

Merci bien, madame, de votre carte, mais vous me feriez beaucoup plus de plaisir, si vous pouviez m'envoyer des types, ce genre de carte, me plaisant plus.

Recevez mes remerciments d'avance, et agréez madame, mes sincères salutations. Adresse : F. Bour Curepipe

Port-Louis. - Le Théâtre

The theatre, horse races at the Mauritius Turf Club, balls held at Government House, the Masonic Lodge Triple Espérance as well as the Catholic Union, fun fairs and charity events – these were all major attractions during the winter months (from June to September) in Port Louis.

Port-Louis - Le Théâtre

Before electricity was installed in 1884, the theatre was lit with lamps filled initially with coconut oil, and later, petrol.

ILE MAURICE. - Le Cimetière des Pères à Sainte-Croix

The cemetery for the missionary priests of the Congregation of Fathers of the Holy Spirit, in Sainte Croix, a northern suburb of Port Louis.

ILE MAURICE. - Le Caveau du Père Laval

In the 1960s a new tomb was built for Father Laval. The old one (shown on this postcard) was too small to accommodate the large number of pilgrims, who came especially around 9 September, the anniversary of his death in 1864.

Father Laval is known as the Apostle of Mauritius. Sent as a French missionary to Mauritius in 1841, he worked with freed slaves, and devoted himself to converting the local population. On his death on 9 September 1864, Father Laval was given the right to have a public funeral.

Father Laval's tomb before 1960 in Sainte Croix.

Réconnaissance des Restes du
Serviteur de Dieu
JACQUES DÉSIRÉ LAVAL

Father Laval was beatified on 23 April 1979 by John Paul II, before leaders of the Mauritian government and the Diocese of Port Louis. The first step, "identifying the corpse", took place on 2 May 1923 in the presence of the bishop of Port Louis, Father Jean-Baptiste Murphy.

ILE MAURICE. - La Foule à l'Entrée du Caveau

A crowd gathers at the entrance to the tomb.

ILE MAURICE. - Le Caveau du Père Laval

Pilgrims of all denominations thronged to visit Father Laval's tomb, their numbers increasing as the anniversary of his death approached.

ILE MAURICE. - La Foule entre l'Église et le Caveau

A crowd in front of Father Laval's tomb, close to the anniversary of his death.

Port-Louis - Cathédrale

The status of the parish church of St Louis was elevated to that of cathedral at the formation of the Catholic Diocese of Port Louis in 1847. It was built in a square between the Champ de Mars and Government House, near to Little Mountain, where Fort Adelaide was located.

Mauritius. La Cathédrale, Port Louis.

St Louis is one of the oldest parish churches in Mauritius, dating from the early 1720s. Its construction was followed by those of Pamplemousses in 1743, and St Pierre and St Julien de Flacq in 1777. After the arrival of the Holy Spirit missionaries in 1847, more Catholic parishes were created, such as those at Poudre d'Or, St Jean and Souillac.

La Cathédrale de Port-Louis, Procession du St Sacrement
Port-Louis Cathedral, Procession of the Holy Sacrament.

Cliché Gentil.

Procession of the Holy Sacrament.

PORT-LOUIS. - Cathédrale St-Louis

Today St Louis is the setting for major liturgical ceremonies, such as processions. However, in the 18th century it was often used by the military and administrative authorities as a warehouse, an arsenal and even barracks. During the French Revolution it served as a meeting room for the colonial assembly. Church services were relocated and held in a vast wooden warehouse situated in the Parc à Boulets at Trou Fanfaron.

15 — La Cathédrale Saint-James (à Port-Louis)

Edition des Magasins Réunis
Reproduction interdite

St Louis was built on unstable foundations and cracks appeared soon after its construction. In 1813, at the instigation of Governor Farquhar, it was rebuilt upon the same foundations. It suffered the same problems, and cracks reappeared. In 1933 Bishop James Leen decided to build a new cathedral using a lighter iron frame.

Anglican St James Cathedral was built upon a former French powder magazine, hence the 3-metre-thick walls. The cathedral was consecrated on 26 June 1850 by the Rt Revd James Chapman, Bishop of Colombo, Sri Lanka.

The interior of St Louis Cathedral was decorated with many paintings by local artists, such as *La Pêche miraculeuse* by Alfred Richard, and with paintings bought from prominent European studios. It was the practice in these studios for the faces of the main characters to be painted by major artists such as Horace Vernet (1789–1863).

ILE MAURICE. - Cathédrale Saint Louis

PORT-LOUIS. - St-James - Cathédrale

Reverend Denny was the first pastor of St James Cathedral. During the conversion of the powder magazine, an elegant colonnaded veranda was added, as well as a tall spire that the residents of Port Louis nicknamed "Denny's tooth-pick".

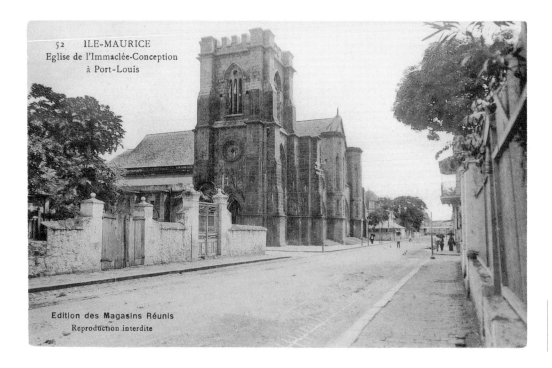

52   ILE-MAURICE
Eglise de l'Immaclée-Conception
à Port-Louis

Edition des Magasins Réunis
Reproduction interdite

On 14 March 1858, the first bishop of Port Louis, the Rt Revd William Allen Collier, split the parish of St Louis, creating a new parish dedicated to the Immaculate Conception.

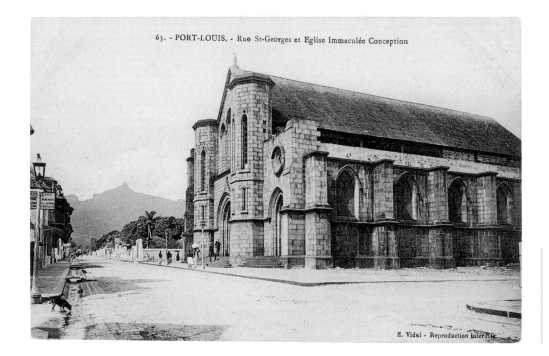

63. - PORT-LOUIS. - Rue St-Georges et Eglise Immaculée Conception

E. Vidal - Reproduction interdite

Bishop William Allen Collier entrusted the Church of the Immaculate Conception to a Belgian priest, Xavier Masuy. Despite his blindness, Masuy, helped by the Mauritian congregation of Notre Dame du Bon et Perpétuel Secours, succeeded in building a massive stone church, at the corner of St Georges Street and Créoles Street (Mere Barthelemy Street today).

Port-Louis - Rue Royale - La Mosquée

The Jummah Mosque was not the first Muslim place of worship on the island. Before 1805, the Muslims had built the al-Aqsa Mosque in Plaine Verte with permission from the French governor Decaen. This was one of the first mosques to be legally built on French territory.

9 **Port-Louis** — La Mosquée

Located far from the town centre, where many Muslim traders were based, the al-Aqsa Mosque was not conveniently located. Therefore, in the mid-19th century the traders decided to build the Jummah Mosque in the heart of the commercial centre of Port Louis.

On 20 October 1852, eight wealthy Muslim merchants decided to build the Jummah Mosque. They bought two plots of land adjacent to Queen and Royal streets, and converted an existing house there into a place of worship. Inaugurated in 1853, it could hold 200 worshippers.

By 1857, a much larger place of worship was required. But the Muslim community had to wait until 1877 for any sign of a new mosque. The leaders of the mosque had bought seven adjoining plots of land. This meant that they owned a third of a hectare in the heart of Port Louis. The worshippers now started to collect funds to build their mosque.

Port Louis. Les Mahométans, en 1re prière dans la Mosquée.

From 1878, Muslim leaders commissioned the best religious architects from India to harmonize the architectural style of the new buildings with that of the old. Leading the architects was Ishaq Mistry.

Port Louis. Les Mahométans en 3me. prière dans la Mosquée.

In 1895, the construction and decoration of the Jummah Mosque was finally completed, and ever since, this architectural marvel has been admired by Mauritians and tourists alike.

Maurice.
Le Baptême du nouveau bassin de la Pagode Indoue
,,Caillasson" ,,Rivière Lataniers".

This postcard shows the inauguration of the Kaylasson temple basins, which were used for ritual ablutions in the Hindu Tamil Sockalingum Mariamen Temple (also known as Kaylasson Temple). The temple is found on Nicolay Road, not far from the Latanier River.

90

Port Louis. ,,Ghoon" Plaine Verte.

14

Celebrating the Yamsé Festival, or Ghoon Festival, in the Muslim district of Plaine Verte, Port Louis.

PORT-LOUIS. – Jardin de la Plaine Verte

The Plaine Verte Garden provides a green belt amongst a concrete jungle between Magon E Street and Sir Edgar Laurent Street. It starts, upstream, at Boulevard Victoria, and ends, downstream, at the junction with Royal Street and its extension, Nicolay Road. It is one of the major venues for political speeches.

3. PORT LOUIS — Square Emilien Ducray. Place de la Pleine vert
Port Louis - Square " Emilien Ducray " " Green Plain "

Cliché G. Rehaut

Émilien-Ducray Square was calm and bucolic in the early 20th century. Renamed Muamar-Kadhafi Square, it is now heavily congested with traffic, especially since it has become the bus terminal. It was here, on 15 April 1882, that the Madagascan Prince Ratsitatane was executed, convicted of supposedly inciting a slave rebellion.

PORT-LOUIS. – Statue de St-Louis
Place de la Cathédrale

In the square of St Louis Cathedral stands an obelisk-shaped fountain filled with water from the Pouce Creek, along with an imitation marble statue of St Louis, King of France. In front of the statue used to be the *dépôt*, consisting of a large stone cross enclosed by an iron railing. Before this cross once stood two cylindrical stones on which coffins were placed while waiting for the pallbearers. Dating probably earlier than the fountain, the stones were removed on 25 August 1947.

Port-Louis - Statue de Brown Séquard

In the East India Company Garden stands a bust of Dr Charles Édouard Brown-Séquard, a native of Mauritius (1817–1894). This world-famous physiologist studied medicine in Paris, and qualified as a doctor in 1846. He settled in the United States in 1852 where he achieved renown after publishing a treatise on obstetrics. Then he held several university chairs, and created a physiology laboratory. He was one of the greatest scientists of his time. The 1924 cyclone damaged the original bust made of imitation marble. The inauguration of the present bust, in bronze, took place in 1928.

The East India Company Garden was initially the 250-metre-wide estuary to the Pouce Creek. It divided the town in two – the Port Louis harbour and commercial centre, and the future Ward IV, the capital's central and western districts. The first inhabitants settled along its banks, while government buildings were erected on the promontory.

50   ILE-MAURICE — Jardin de la Compagnie à Port-Louis

Edition des Magasins Réunis
Reproduction interdite

93

Around 1771, there was a market at this spot, which was later moved to the site where the theatre now stands, only to be relocated here after the fire of 1816. Governor Colville decided to transform this plot of land into a public garden, and had trees planted. Those same trees can still be admired today.

21. - PORT-LOUIS (Ile Maurice). - Jardin de la Compagnie
Cliché E. Gentil Fils   45   Collection A. Béchard & Cⁱᵉ — Reproduction interdite

Port-Louis - Jardin de la Compagnie

This statue of Adrien d'Épinay stands in the East India Company Garden. This tribute to him provoked some controversy, as he was considered an advocate of slavery. However, the statue has been granted protection as a historical monument.

3 — **Port-Louis** - Company's Garden

Adrien d'Épinay (1794–1839), lawyer and politician, is one of the most important men in Mauritian history. To his critics, he represented all that was wrong with the privileged Franco-Mauritian oligarchy. Despite being very few in number, these families dominated Mauritius's economy, politics and even the British civil service for over a century (1840–1948).

Le Square Thomy Pitot et le Square d'Adrien d'Epinay, Port-Louis.
Thomy Pitot and Adrien d'Épinay Squares, Port-Louis.   Cliché Gentil.

Adrien d'Épinay became a barrister on 28 December 1821, and successfully defended a captain who was accused of taking part in the illegal slave trade. From then on he was regarded as the political leader of Franco-Mauritian colonists.

9. Port Louis. Statue de d'Epinay.

On 25 January 1827, Adrien d'Épinay created the National Committee for the Defence of the Interests of the Mauritian Plantocracy. He won the right for colonists to serve on the Legislative Council, established the first bank, lifted press censorship, and founded the first free and uncensored newspaper in Mauritius. He also negotiated and obtained compensation on behalf of slave owners for the loss of their slaves – something his critics could never forgive him for. The money was used to modernize the Mauritian sugar industry.

20 MAURITIUS. Place de l'Immigration. — Immigration Square. Port-Louis.

Édition J. Grancourt et Cie - Tous droits réservés.

Immigration Square was named after the half a million Indian agricultural labourers who worked in the Mauritian sugar industry. Half chose to settle in Mauritius rather than return to India. Their descendants now account for about 70 per cent of the Mauritian population.

6 -- Place de l'Immigration (Port-Louis)

Edition des Magasins Réunis
Reproduction interdite

On 12 July 2002, UNESCO recognized the Immigration Depot, or *Aapravasi Ghat* in Hindi, as a World Heritage site. This building complex processed the indentured workforce arriving from India, as well as slaves, mainly from Africa.

Desforges Street linked Plaine Verte to the town hall. It was named after Governor Antoine Marie Desforges-Boucher of Réunion, who opened this road for traffic around 1765.

Rue Desforges, Port-Louis
Desforges Street, Port-Louis

Cliché Gentil

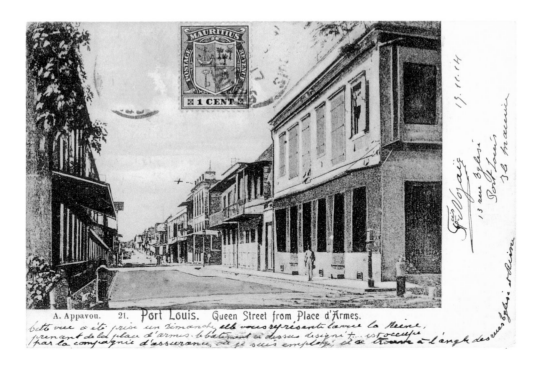

Queen Street was named after Queen Victoria, but actually dates from the 18th century. In fact, after the French Revolution, it was named rue de Nancy.

A. Appavou.   21. Port Louis.   Queen Street from Place d'Armes.

Port-Louis - Rue de l'Arsenal - La Citadelle

Arsenal Road starts from the Trou Fanfaron police station, and ends at the foot of the eastern side of Little Mountain, on top of which Fort Adelaide perches.

··98

PORT-LOUIS. - Rue Farquhar

Sir Robert Townsend Farquhar Road, named after the first British governor, runs parallel to Quay Road, Queen Street and Royal Street. Once the main commercial artery of the town, today it suffers from its proximity to two municipal markets.

Hospital Road was so named because it did indeed lead to the civilian hospital situated on the quays, until 1899. This road, shown on the postcard, and bordering the west side of Jummah Mosque, was renamed Louis Pasteur Street in 1923.

99

The building on the left in this postcard showing the Place du Quai dates from the period of French colonial rule in the 18th century. It is *waqf* (i.e. a religious endowment in Islamic law) and is known today as the Money Changers Building.

68. - PORT-LOUIS. - Rue du Rempart

E. Vidal - Reproduction interdite

Rempart Street with the Vidal store on the left. "Rempart" refers to the basalt promontory carved out by the Ruisseau du Pouce. A stone wall held back the left river bank. Beyond this "rempart" stood some beautiful houses.

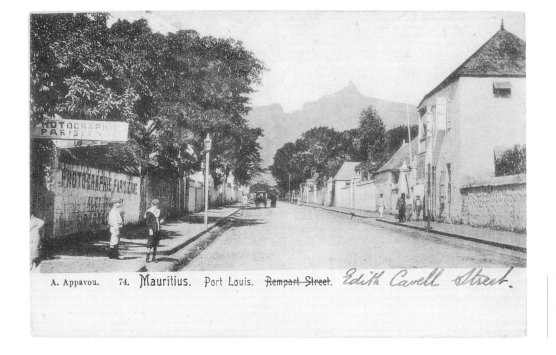

A. Appavou. 74. Mauritius. Port Louis. Rempart Street. Edith Cavell Street.

Rempart Street was renamed Edith Cavell Street in 1917, after a British member of the Belgian Resistance during the First World War. Edith Cavell, born in 1865 and a dedicated nurse and patriot, was executed by the Germans in 1915.

The intersection of Chaussée Street, Rempart Street (Edith Cavell Street today) and Barracks Road. On the left stands the A. Mautalent store, one of the best places to shop in Port Louis before the First World War.

Royal Street is half Chinese and half Muslim. The atmosphere changes just by walking into another shop, or by crossing from one side of the street to the other. There is no rivalry between the different cultures and they manage to live side by side in perfect harmony.

PORT-LOUIS (1892). - Rue de la Chaussée

A. Rambert - Cliché réservé

Chaussée Street was laid on the city's former marshlands, which were reclaimed by the French.

89. - PORT-LOUIS 1909. - Rue de la Chaussée

E. Vidal - Reproduction interdite

Originally this causeway joining Government House to the Central Barracks was used mainly by the military. However, after civilians reclaimed Chaussée Street for themselves, it rapidly turned into one of the main shopping streets of Port Louis.

Edition des Magasins Réunis
Reproduction interdite

42 — ILE-MAURICE - Place d'Armes - Port-Louis

The Place d'Armes harkens back to the Port Louis of Governor La Bourdonnais. Back then, it was the parade and exercise grounds for the military, with Government House and the port at the ends. On its sides, Place d'Armes opened out onto the guardhouse, prison, general stores, warehouses, War Office, Registry, chapel and armoury.

PORT-LOUIS. - La Place d'Armes le 18 Juin 1909

The Place du Quai, 18 June 1909. Capitalists and conservatives were hostile to the Royal Commissioners who had come to investigate the finances of the sugar industry. The Reformists and Democrats, supported by agricultural workers, were, on the other hand, in favour of the investigation.

Entrée du Bazar

The central market of Port Louis is today situated on the estuary of a dried-up creek. Before, there were many boats anchored here, which had to be locked up to prevent them from being stolen by slaves hoping to reach Madagascan or African soil.

Audusson et Vidal. — Mauritius

Port-Louis. *Le Bazar*

The "bazaar", the market of Port Louis, situated between Queen Street and Sir Robert Townsend Farquhar Street, was built between 1839 and 1845. It was the work of master-builder John Augustus Lloyd, who arrived in Mauritius in 1831, and who contributed many other buildings to the island's architectural heritage.

Port Louis. Entrance gate of the central Market.

Before finally settling on the current site, the market was first located in front of the former St Louis Church, at the corner of Royal Street and Sir William Newton Street. It was moved to the spot where the theatre was later to be built, and subsequently close to the East India Company Garden.

Port-Louis - Rue de la Reine - Les Bazars

A wide variety of vegetables, fruits, household and religious objects was offered to the island's multi-cultural population, which originated from different continents (Europe, Africa and Asia), adhered to different religions (Christianity, Hinduism, Islam, Buddhism), and spoke a number of different languages.

Rue Pope Henessy. (Port-Louis)

Pope Hennessy Street was also known as Government Street because it linked the Champs de Mars to Government House. This postcard seems to portray the return of the procession of the Holy Sacrament, marking the feast of Corpus Christi. The followers were heading to St Louis Cathedral, having visited the altar or Reposoir, traditionally erected on the Champs de Mars.

Mauritius

Pope Hennessy Street

Sir John Pope Hennessy was known in Mauritius for his gubernatorial motto "Mauritius for the Mauritians". He backed the Mauritian reformers who wanted to elect representatives to defend their interests. In May 1884, Lord Derby, State Secretary of the Colonies, consented to the proposition. The first elections to the legislative council took place in January 1886.

The 15th British governor of Mauritius, Sir John Pope Hennessy, was the first Catholic Member of Parliament and was elected in 1859. Called to the bar in 1861, he became, in 1867, the governor of Labuan, off Sabah, in East Malaysia today. Pope Hennessy subsequently became governor of the Gold Coast (Ghana today) in 1872, the Bahamas in 1873, the Windward Islands in 1875 and Hong Kong in 1877. He spoke up for the Africans of Ghana and the black population of the Windward Islands, to the dismay of sugar planters and colonial officials. In 1882, he was nominated to be governor of New South Wales in Australia, but his nomination was strongly opposed, and was quickly withdrawn.

A. Appavou.   75. Mauritius. Port Louis. Pope Hennessy Street.

Sir John Pope Hennessy took the post of governor of Mauritius in 1883, and landed on the island on 1 June. In a short time he had antagonized the head of the Admiralty, the Catholic Bishop William Benoît Scarisbrick (1828–1908), and a large number of British colonial officials. The latter accused him of siding with the Mauritians in their disputes with officialdom.

Rue Pope Henessy et la Place du Théâtre, Port-Louis.
Pope Henessy street and the Theatre Square, Port-Louis.

Cliché Gentil.

Port~Louis~Mauritius. ~ Pope Hennessy Street

The National Hotel on Pope Hennessy Street was considered, for many years, one of the best restaurants in Port Louis. It was made famous by the poet and painter Malcolm de Chazal, who frequented it whenever he was in Port Louis. This was where he wrote a large part of his work, and painted a large number of watercolours.

SCENERY PORT LOUIS, MAURITIUS

The title of this postcard "Scenery Port Louis" is misleading. Carts, especially those pulled by cattle, were more likely to be seen in rural areas, where they were used to transport sugar cane. In towns, it was more usual to see carriages and wagons pulled by mules or men. A large number of rural carts at Port Louis normally indicated a public meeting, the presence of a famous visitor or a religious festival.

The arrival of the first automobiles on the island was a noteworthy event. The first car arrived on 28 January 1901 on the steamer *Iraouady*.

The Epargne and Maurice banks face each other at the corner of Place d'Armes, Chaussée Street and Intendance.

Rue Cattle Walk, Cyclone du 29 Avril 1892.

Cliché Alex Rambert, Maurice.

Magasin Ste Anne
38, Rue de l'Eglise.

This postcard shows Cattle Walk Street in the wake of the cyclone of 29 April 1892. It was a particularly destructive and deadly hurricane and many Mauritians in the early 20th century calculated how old they were by remembering their respective ages at the time of the storm.

Rue Madame, Cyclone du 29 Avril 1892.

Cliché Alex Rambert, Maurice.

Magasin Ste Anne
38, Rue de l'Eglise.

Madame Street in the wake of the cyclone of 29 April 1892. The toll was heavy: 600 dead, a thousand injured, and 3,000 homes destroyed.

Cliché Alex Rambert, Maurice.

Tombeau-Malartic, Champs de Mars, Cyclone du 29 Avril 1892.

Magasin Ste Anne
38, Rue de l'Eglise.

At Champ de Mars, even part of the obelisk on Malartic's tomb was destroyed. This gives an idea of how strong the gusts were during the cyclone of 29 April 1892.

Cliché Alex Rambert, Maurice.

Rue du Gouvernement, Cyclone du 29 Avril 1892.

Magasin Ste Anne
38, Rue de l'Eglise.

Government Street in the wake of the cyclone of 29 April 1892. The cyclone was exceptional because it struck at the end of summer. In Mauritius, cyclones generally occur from mid-December to late March. Also, the speed of the cyclone on 29 April 1892 was the greatest that had ever been recorded.

La Rade de PORT-LOUIS

E. Vidal – Reproduction interdite

In the days before air travel, it was an enchanting experience to arrive in the morning at Port Louis by ship. Early risers would be rewarded with the magnificent panorama of the Moka mountains as they entered Port Louis harbour.

La Rade de PORT-LOUIS

E. Vidal - Reproduction interdite

A. Apparou.   18.   Port Louis.   View of the harbour.

8   Port-Louis

77. - PORT-LOUIS. - Bureaux du Port

E. Vidal. Reproduction interdite

Régates à Port-Louis
Regattas at Port-Louis

Cliché Gentil

70. - PORT-LOUIS. - Débarquement de Bœufs de Madagascar

E. Vidal - Reproduction interdite

Débarquement des Bœufs

CENTRAL

Central Mauritius comprises two distinct geographical areas: the urban west and the rural east. The urban part snakes up from Curepipe in the south to the outskirts of Port Louis in the north. In the late 19th century, after successive epidemics of cholera, smallpox, malaria and the plague (and other diseases), the inhabitants fled the capital and the mosquito-infected coastal regions, and took refuge in Plaines Wilhems and the western district of Moka – regions considered to be healthier.

The construction of the railway in the early 1860s accelerated this exodus, since it made moving to the epidemic-free regions easier. For some reason, this railway did not follow the same route as the previous French railway, which connected Mahébourg to Port Louis via Riche-en-Eau, Pavé Citron, Quartier Militaire and Pamplemousses. Instead it went in the direction of the new Mahébourg/Port-Louis road via Rose Belle, Curepipe and Rose Hill, through primary forests, and bordering, sometimes spanning, deep ravines and fast flowing rivers along the Grande Rivière Nord-Ouest.

The highlands, especially Curepipe, though originally swampy, attracted the wealthiest families from the coastal areas and the capital. From the 1860s, these newly established regions grew into towns. Newcomers set to work dismantling beautiful wooden houses in remote locations, and rebuilding them in the centre of Curepipe. The most stunning example is its town hall. Formerly Malmaison de Moka, it was relocated from St Pierre and rebuilt on the site of the former Mare aux Songes, the birthplace of the city. Just a year, almost to the day, after the laying of the foundation stone of the new town hall on 4 February 1902 by Governor Charles Bruce, it was opened with great fanfare.

The Royal Navy, whose sailors, stationed in coastal areas, were severely affected by malaria, built large barracks on the western highlands of Curepipe. However, after the discovery of typhoid in the city's wells they went on to construct new buildings at Vacoas, which was supplied with chlorinated water from the La Mare aux Vacoas reservoir, through the filtering station at La Marie.

The newly settled population of wealthy families and soldiers in Curepipe and Vacoas were joined by other settlers, from the middle class and lower income groups – workmen, agricultural workers, artisans, farmers, gardeners, small proprietors and employees. These people were happy to settle in the suburbs and outskirts of the wealthy districts, and chose areas such as Engrais Martial, Camp Fouquereaux, Clairfonds, Solférino, Bonne Terre and Glen Park.

The Basses Plaines Wilhems, Quatre Bornes, Beau Bassin and its sister town Rose Hill were home to the majority of Britons. Many senior British diplomats set their sights on the most beautiful plots in Beau Bassin, especially those along the deep ravine of Plaines Wilhems. The region is also conveniently close to the capital and administrative centre. The most notable example of British settlement in the region is Llewellyn Castle, where the young naturalist Charles Darwin stayed as a guest of state engineer C.A. Lloyd in 1836. At the end of the 20th century, Llewellyn Castle became first a Mt Tabor spiritual centre before eventually being taken over by the Catholic Diocese of Port Louis.

It was not just the proximity of the capital that led British officials to choose Beau Bassin over Curepipe. Beau Bassin also enjoys a more temperate climate than

Le Parc du Réduit

The gardens at Château du Réduit.

Le Pouce et le Peterboth, vue de Moka
The Pouce and Peterboth mountains

Cliché Gueil

CUREPIPE CAMP
MAURITIUS

TOP: The Moka mountains, just visible in the distance, flank the Moka plain. Here, the highlands enjoy a temperate climate, but the other side descends into the blazing heat of Port Louis.

ABOVE: Military exercises in the barracks located southwest of Curepipe.

Port Louis, which has hot summers, and Curepipe, which is almost constantly drowned in rain and fog throughout the year. Beau Bassin furthermore has an abundance of fruit trees and flowers. One can spend pleasant evenings outdoors even in winter.

The Basses Plaines Wilhems was originally home to plantations – Cascade, Beau Bassin, Montroches, Roches Brunes, Plaisance, Stanley, Rose Hill, Beau Sejour, La Louise were sugar factories before becoming suburban and urban neighbourhoods. Another example is Camp Levieux, named in honour of the surveyor of the same name. The sprawling urban districts of St Jean and Sodnac did not exist before 1960. When cyclones Alix and Carol ravaged the island in January and February of that year, sugar cane fields still lined St Jean Road, between the market town of Quatre Bornes and the crossroads of St Jean, Royal and Réduit roads, up to the church and the cemetery of St Jean. From the 1960s, hundreds of new inhabitants, mostly officials, flocked to the districts of St Jean and Sodnac every year. The days of sugar cane forming a green belt separating Vacoas from Quatre Bornes were numbered: the parcelling, settlement and urbanization of Candos Hill were imminent.

The rural regions of the centre of Mauritius are very different from each other. Winds from the east bring rain, but also cooler temperatures. Continuously assaulted by winds, the water in the lagoon is healthier than the stagnant waters found in the West (Black River) and the North. The eastern lagoons (Belle Mare, Trou d'Eau Douce, Roches Noires) shimmer in a thousand different colours in the sunshine, from the blinding white of the beaches and the sapphire shades of the sea, to the striking emerald of the deepest basins.

Here unfold the swathes of brilliant verdant sugarcane fields, belonging to Beau-Champ and FUEL, the only factories remaining today in what was once the heartland of the sugar cane industry, with up to 88 sugar plantations in just two districts.

The districts of Moka and Flacq are enchanting. Moka is cooler than Flacq, sunnier but subject to heavy rain and widespread flooding. The landscape slopes gently into the horizon, reaching only up to four to five hundred metres from sea level over a distance of 30 kilometres. The view is often magnificent, with a beautiful mosaic of colours. It is unforgettable in May, at dawn, when the sugar cane fields sparkle in the rays of the rising sun.

In contrast, this easy laid-back lifestyle is scarce in the Black River savannah and the burning plains of Yémen, La Gaulette, La Mecque, Gros Cailloux and the parched Albion. Here the rugged scenery stretches out under a blazing sun. Once regarded as the poorest region of Mauritius, the Black River has become a tourist mecca, attracting tens of thousands of foreign visitors – sun seekers, anglers and hunters for deer. It is also a haven for water sports, surfing and golf, which can be played at the foot of Le Morne or Montagne du Rempart. Malaria was eradicated in 1948 due to the use of powerful but polluting DDT, and now there is a steady influx of wealthy families building beautiful homes on the slopes of Tourelle du Tamarin, Rempart and Piton de la Petite Rivière, transforming this former wasteland into lush gardens and blossoming orchards.

10 — **Cure-pipe** - Entrée du Jardin Botanique

On 26 August 1867, the government acquired some land for the cultivation of the cinchona tree, from which quinine, a remedy for malaria, is extracted. As more land was acquired and the site expanded, the Curepipe Botanic Gardens was born.

The volcanic crater of Trou aux Cerfs.

29. - Ile Maurice. - Le Marché de Curepipe

The former Curepipe town market was built in the late 19th century by Fébure Martial following plans drawn up by the cartographer Descubes. The building was completed on 23 April 1879.

10. MAURITIUS. Marché de Curepipe — Curepipe Market.

Édition J. Grancourt et Cie - Tous droits réservés,

Market day in Curepipe, in the former town market.

13. ~ Curepipe. ~ Le Marché

The Curepipe market was destroyed by Cyclone Carol, sometime between 27 February and 1 March 1960.

Camp Indien à Curepipe

The Central Printing Establi. Ile Maurice

Farmland on the outskirts of Curepipe.

Hôtel de Ville, Curepipe
Town Hall at Curepipe.

Cliché Gentil.

Governor Charles Bruce laid the foundation stone for the town hall of Curepipe on 4 February 1902. This colonial-style building was once a beautiful wooden house in St Pierre called "La Malmaison de Moka", which was dismantled, brought to Curepipe and rebuilt on this site.

39   ILE-MAURICE — Statue de Paul et Virginie - Hôtel de Ville - Curepipe

Edition des Magasins Réunis
Reproduction interdite

In July 1902, a group of statues by Prosper d'Épinay (1836–1914), a Mauritian sculptor living in Europe, was placed in the town hall gardens.

ILE-MAURICE — Hôtel de Ville de Curepipe

Edition des Magasins Réunis
Reproduction interdite

In Europe, Prosper d'Épinay had a reputation as "the sculptor of crowned heads". His statue of Edward VII was erected on 24 July 1912 on the Champs de Mars esplanade, Port Louis.

135

56   ILE-MAURICE — Le Lac de l'Hôtel de Ville à Curepipe

Edition des Magasins Réunis
Reproduction interdite

A view of the lake at the town hall of Curepipe.

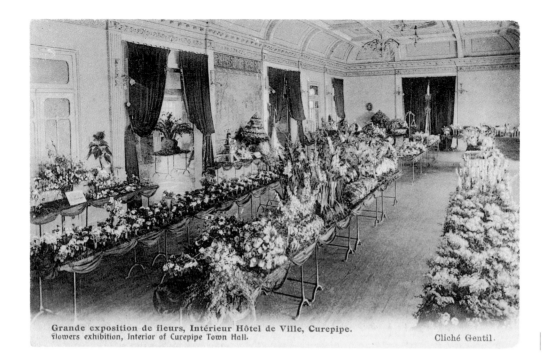

Grande exposition de fleurs, Intérieur Hôtel de Ville, Curepipe.
flowers exhibition, Interior of Curepipe Town Hall.

Cliché Gentil.

A flower show held at the town hall of
Curepipe.

136

A. Appavou. 40. Mauritius. Curepipe-Townhall.

Curepipe town hall as seen from the
former train station, now the bus station.

11. – Vue panoramique de Curepipe

A view of the Curepipe town hall from the belfry of the parish church of St Thérèse d'Avila, with the roof of the former convent of Notre Dame du Bon Secours in the foreground.

The Château Mallac was converted into the Park Hotel in the 1950s. It was here that the tourism and hospitality industry of Maurice was born.

30. - CUREPIPE (Ile Maurice). - Le Magasin Guillemin

C. Guillemin and Co. was opened to the public on 1 November 1912 by brothers Emmanuel and Claudius Guillemin. Built by the architect Maurice Loumeau, it was the most stunning shopping complex in Mauritius before independence.

Taken from the first floor of C. Guillemin and Co., now Arcade Currimjee, this photograph shows the eastern end of the Royal College Curepipe. Across the street was the two-storeyed Merven building. Built with reinforced concrete, it was an architectural marvel of its time.

60   ILE-MAURICE — Route du Jardin et Family Hôtel à Curepipe

Edition des Magasins Réunis
- Reproduction interdite

In this postcard, we see, from left to right, the Family Hotel, which C. Guillemin and Co. later became, the Route du Jardin (Winston Churchill Street today) and the south side of Royal College Curepipe.

61   ILE-MAURICE — Route du Jardin et Succursale des Magasins Réunis à Curepipe

AUX MAGASINS REUNIS

Edition des Magasins Réunis
Reproduction interdite

The Curepipe branch of Aux Magasins Réunis on the Route du Jardin, down the road from C. Guillemin and Co.

A drawing by the painter Xavier Le Juge de Segrais of a Curepipe stream flowing through the area aptly named Eau Coulée (Running Water).

The World War I Memorial was inaugurated on 15 April 1922. It consists of a French infantryman and a British "Tommy" holding up the laurels of Victory.

11. MAURITIUS. Collège Royal et Monument de la — Royal College and Great war
Grande Guerre. Memorial. Curepipe.

Édition J. Grancourt et Cie – Tous droits réservés.

The Royal College Curepipe was destroyed and rebuilt twice, the first time between 1887 and 1888, and the second in 1912 to accommodate the ever-increasing number of students.

57 — ILE-MAURICE - Le Collège Royal à Curepipe

Edition des Magasins Réunis
Reproduction interdite

Another view of Royal College Curepipe. The absence of the 1914–1918 War Memorial in the photograph indicates that the postcard dates prior to 1922.

142

26. ~ Curepipe. - Eglise Sainte-Thérèse

19. MAURITIUS. Église Sainte-Hélène. "Curepipe Road".
Sainte-Helena Church "Curepipe Road".

Édition J, Grancourt et Cie - Tous droits réservés.

The façade of the parish church of St Thérèse d'Avila, whose spire rises to 46 metres.

During the opening of the Basilica St Hélène on 21 August 1927, the bishop of Port-Louis, Bishop Jacques Leen, acknowledged the generosity of Héléna Naz, the daughter of Sir Virgile Naz, who was a major donor towards the building of the church.

27. ~ Curepipe. ~ Eglise Sainte-Hélène

The architect for the Basilica St Hélène was André Gaillardin, who was a graduate of the École des Beaux Arts in Paris. In Neo-Romanesque style, the building was characterized by semi-circular arches. The church took the shape of a cross, with a dome capping the intersection of the arms. The construction of the basilica took over four years.

143

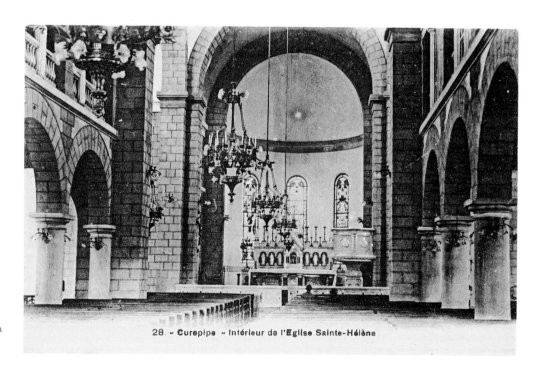

28. ~ Curepipe ~ Intérieur de l'Eglise Sainte-Hélène

The interior of the Basilica St Hélène. Reinforced concrete was used to build the vaults and domes, and 27 tonnes of Carrara marble used for the altars, pulpit, communion tables and statues.

Curepipe

Sainte-Thérèse

The history of the Church of St Thérèse d'Avila starts with its first priest, Father Pierre Michael Comerford. He used his own money to buy the large piece of land that now comprises the parish of St Thérèse, Lorette Convent and St Joseph College.

Paysage, Curepipe
Landscape, Curepipe

Cliché Gentil

A view of the Church of St Thérèse d'Avila from the gardens of the Curepipe town hall. In 1864, the nuns of Notre Dame du Bon Secours made the journey every day from Belle Rose to Curepipe to teach the children attending primary school here.

58 — ILE-MAURICE - Eglise Sainte-Thérèse à Curepipe

Edition des Magasins Réunis
Reproduction interdite

The parish church of St Thérèse was modified and extended several times. The foundation stone was first laid on 6 September 1869, but the French architect, Rampan, later refused categorically to revise his architectural plans and departed, taking them with him. However, Virgile Naz had memorized them and managed to complete the church, with the assistance of Bruniquel, a builder.

Paysage, Curepipe
Landscape, Curepipe

Cliché Gentil

A view from the former train station of Curepipe, looking across to the bell tower of St Thérèse d'Avila over the town hall gardens.

Eglise Ste Thérèse à Curepipe

The Central Printing Estabt: Ile Maurice:

A sketch by Xavier Le Juge de Segrais showing the parish church of St Thérèse, still without its spire.

On 15 February 1904, the parish of St Thérèse decided to enlarge the church because the new marble altar, commissioned by Father O'Loughlin, was too tall for the choir vault. In 1922, the front of the church was widened by 4.5 metres in order to erect the present façade. It was designed by architect Paul Marion du Procé.

Consulat de France — Curepipe

A view of the residence of the Consul of France in Curepipe. Many Mauritian diplomats have held this honorary post in Mauritius since 1840.

Audusson et Vidal — Mauritius

Curepipe — Vélodrome

Opened in 1902, Curepipe velodrome was one of the best sports facilities in Mauritius, though spectators had to bring their own chairs with their names written on them. Today, it is the Winston Churchill Football Stadium.

A view of a gazebo in the Curepipe Botanic Gardens, established in the late 19ᵗʰ century.

The Botanic Gardens harken back to Curepipe's origins. The territory was first granted as a concession to Pierre Colas de Berville on 6 January 1757. Named Mare aux Joncs (Reed Pond), it went on to have many different owners before being partitioned. This was how Curepipe began as a settlement.

40   ILE-MAURICE — Délicieux site au Jardin Botanique - Curepipe

Edition des Magasins Réunis
Reproduction interdite

The Commercial Gazette of 18 August 1865 suggested that a botanic garden should be set up at Curepipe for those varieties of plants that could not withstand the hot climate of the Pamplemousses region. To help get the project started, one of the proprietors of Mare aux Joncs, Alphonse Lucas, offered a piece of land to the Mauritian government on 26 August 1868.

CUREPIPE. - Pont au Jardin Botanique

E. Vidal. - Reproduction interdite

The Botanic Gardens started to take shape. In December 1869, the government acquired approximately 15.42 hectares for planting cinchonas. In 1890, Curepipe officially obtained town status, and an urban council took partial control of the garden. Those in charge of the project were, in turn, Fernand Bijoux, Charles O'Connor, Henri Bestel and Jacques Lamalétie.

CUREPIPE. - Bassin bleu

E. Vidal - Reproduction interdite

As many rivers pass through it, Curepipe is very marshy. During cyclones, many homes suffer from flooding.

E. Vidal - Reproduction interdite   73. - CUREPIPE. - Pont Sir Virgile Naz

The Virgile Naz Bridge pays tribute to a Mauritian politician, who was the owner of Château Belvédère. He also owned a property at the foot of Trou aux Cerfs, bordered by two Curepipe rivers – the Sèche and the Gros Cerfs.

CUREPIPE. - Bassin Naz

E. Vidal. - Reproduction interdite

A pond formed by one of the Curepipe rivers.

E. Vidal - Reproduction interdite

74. - CUREPIPE. - Route de Mangalkhan

The Route de Mangalkhan, which links Vacoas to Curepipe, was once lined with pine trees. It was opened in 1892 at the request of George Robinson, a planter and politician.

Curepipe's military hospital, built in the 19th century for malaria-stricken soldiers.

152

The Route Royale in Curepipe runs from the railway station on Curepipe Road towards the Royal College Curepipe and St Thérèse Church.

A Curepipe landscape free from concrete.

153

The roundabout at the junction of Route Royale, Route du Jardin and Rue Chasteauneuf.

CUREPIPE. - Trou-aux-Cerfs

CUREPIPE. - Trou-aux-Cerfs

E. Vidal - Reproduction interdite

CUREPIPE. - Vue du Trou-aux-Cerfs

CUREPIPE. - Vue du Trou-aux-Cerfs

Panoramic views of Trou aux Cerfs. At the bottom of the crater there is a small spring-fed lake, where the deer in the region used to drink.

CUREPIPE. - Fond du Cratère - Trou aux Cerfs

E. Vidal - Reproduction interdite

The English navigator and explorer Matthew Flinders (1774–1814) visited Mauritius and landed at Baie du Cap on 15 December 1803. Governor Decaen kept him under arrest in Mauritius until early 1810. During his captivity he was amongst the first to observe and describe Trou aux Cerfs.

CUREPIPE. - Trou aux Cerfs - Lac au fond du Cratère

Since the early 19th century, there have been numerous descriptions of Trou aux Cerfs crater. One of these came from Captain Palmer, who built Royal Road which connected Port Louis with Mahébourg via Curepipe. Another came from Melchior Bourbon, in his account of his excursion to Trou aux Cerfs in 1853.

A. Appavou.   47.   **Mauritius.** Moka Railway Station.
Discharging sugar canes, embarking sugar.

On 1 November 1880, Governor John Bowen opened the railway from Rose Hill to Grande Rivière Sud-Est. This postcard shows the unloading of sugar cane and loading of sugar at Moka station.

Terrible collision arrivée au Chemin de fer pendant la nuit du 6 Octobre 1909 entre RICHELIEU et COROMANDEL (Ile Maurice)

The photographer of this picture, a Mr Gentil, wrote in October 1909, "This is one of the few accidents that has occurred since the opening of the railway. A freight train from Moka had pulled out of Richelieu and was heading for Port Louis around midnight, when another train from Savane, without slowing down since it left Vacaos, crashed into the back of it. There were at least three mechanics seriously injured."

On 12 September 1932, upon arriving at Richelieu station, a sugar train travelling from Rose Hill to Port Louis collided with an oncoming locomotive, and was derailed.

A drawing of the Château du Reduit by Xavier Le Juge de Segrais. On 27 June 1747, Governor Barthélemy David paid a visit to the Moka region. He realized that this inland region, difficult to access, was an ideal place to build a refuge for women and children in case of British attack.

Audusson et Vidal — Mauritius

Moka — *Le Réduit*

On 26 October 1767, Governor Jean-Daniel Dumas (1767–1768) claimed Château du Réduit as his residence in the name of the King of France.

Le Réduit

On 25 March 1770, the former governor of Madras was the first important guest to visit Château du Réduit. Others followed, the most celebrated amongst them being Mohandas Karamchand, better known as Mahatma Gandhi (1869–1948), in October 1901.

Varangue du Réduit. ~ MAURICE

The veranda of Château du Réduit, circa 1908. A décor of foliage, vines and green plants helped to maintain cool temperatures under the veranda overlooking the gardens.

A. Appavou. 83. Mauritius. Scenery french Gardens „Le Réduit".

The garden of Château du Réduit is one of the acclimatization gardens in Mauritius. From 1764, Governor Desforges-Boucher had 4,000 oak trees planted, as well as chestnut trees, European and tropical fruit trees, and a cinnamon plant that adapted wonderfully well.

4. MAURITIUS Collège d'Agriculture. — Agricultural College "Réduit".

Edition J. Grancourt et Cie - Tous droits réservés.

The study of agriculture in Réduit began with the laying of the foundation stone of the Mauritius College of Agriculture on 2 July 1923.

Collège d'Agriculture du Réduit. (Port-Louis)

The College of Agriculture was completed in 1925 and opened on 12 March in the same year. It was the first institution of higher education in Mauritius and the birthplace of the island's university, established in the 1960s.

Lac au Réduit

The creation of the Station Agronomique at Réduit in 1893, under the auspices of the Department of Agriculture, as well as that of the Mauritius Sugar Industry Research Institute in 1953, added to the already impressive reputation of the Réduit gardens in botany and research.

161

3. MAURITIUS. Pont "Hesketh–Bell". — "Hesketh–Bell" bridge. "Réduit".

A landscape often captured by Mauritian painters: a waterfall with the Hesketh-Bell Bridge (named after the 21st governor of Maurice from 1916 to 1924, Sir Henry Hesketh Bell) mirrored in clear, still waters.

Édition J. Grancourt et Cie - Tous droits réservés.

A. Appavou.   48. **Mauritius.**   Cascade of Le Reduit.

Moka — *Pont du Réduit*

Réduit Cascade, where "Major" Amode
Ibrahim Atchia built a central hydroelectric
plant.

The hydroelectric plant at Réduit Cascade
supplied electricity for several surrounding
villages.

A. Appavou.   6.   Moka.   Waterfall of Reduit.

"Major" Atchia and his brothers built much more than just a hydroelectric plant. They modernized Mauritius by building a foundry, a cinema and a football stadium.

163

12 — Moka - Reduit Bridge

Another view of Réduit Cascade, spanned by a bridge of the same name.

1. MAURITIUS. Route du " Réduit ". — Road to "Réduit" Governor's Residence.

Édition J. Grancourt et Cie - Tous droits réservés.

A view of the road leading from Réduit to Port Louis via Moka. Commuters use the Hesketh-Bell Bridge to cross a tributary of the Grande Rivière Nord-Ouest.

A. Appavou. 41. Mauritius. Souillac Bridge — Moka

Souillac Bridge at Moka.

Mauritius. St. Pierre ès-lien Church-Moka.

WATERFALL AT LES PAILLES. G. MOLLIÈRES.
LA CASCADE DES PAILLES. COPYRIGHT.

The foundations of the parish church of St Pierre ès Liens were laid after those of Port Louis and Grand Port in 1722, Pamplemousses in 1743, and St Pierre and St Julien in 1773.

This waterfall at Pailles is symbolic of La Bourdonnais' efforts to supply Port Louis with running water. During a walk, he realized that the water from the waterfall could be diverted towards the town using the natural slope of the ground.

A. Appavou. 55. Moka "La Laura" Sugar estate during the crop & Peterboth Mountain.

La Laura sugar estate, with the peak of Pieter Both in the background. This picture gives an idea of what the small sugar estates looked like in the early 20th century. They came and went, since business hiccups often led to bankruptcy.

Propriété sucrière „La Laura"
La Laura sugar Estate, Peterboth

Cliché Gentil

A view of the La Laura sugar plantation. This estate was also known as Pieter Both, or Château Tremblant.

3 — Labourage d'un Champ de Cannes - Etablissement Sans-Souci

Edition des Magasins Réunis
Reproduction interdite

Ploughing a sugar cane field. Before 1975, most Mauritians thought that it would be impossible to remove all the basalt rocks scattered in the fields.

CREVE COEUR

PPS/824

A view of Pieter Both (*at left*) towering above Moka plain.

Mauritius. „Peter Booth" Mountain.

If one were to create a Mauritian mythology, the mountains would have to be the leading characters. Pieter Both becomes more and more impressive the closer you get to it. This huge ball of basalt balancing on a natural obelisk is indeed a fascinating sight to behold.

Indian Huts - Pieter-Both

Pieter Both was named after a Dutch admiral who perished in a shipwreck off the shores of Flic-en-Flac on 10 February 1615. The Dutch gave his name to the peak situated to the east of his tomb, otherwise known as Montagne du Rempart.

Pic du Corps de Garde - Plaines Williem

A. Appavou. 76. Mauritius. Peter Both Mountain.

Pieter Both is 828 metres tall. The knife-maker Claude Peuthé was the first to climb it on 8 September 1790. At his side was a porter laden with bows, arrows, strings of various thicknesses, wattle and other tools and materials.

This first ascent was successful due to the ingenuity of Claude Peuthé. An arrow, which was tied to a thick rope with a string, was shot over the basalt top of Pieter Both. The rope, firmly wedged, enabled Claude Peuthé to scale the summit. Once at the top, he dug a hole in the rock to plant the French flag.

4 — Vallée des Prêtres and Peterboth Montain

In 1832, Captain J.A. Lloyd climbed Pieter Both, accompanied by several officers. They claimed to be the first to scale its summit. Lislet Geoffroy, son of a settler and freed slave (Niama, a princess of Senegal), discredited this claim by showing them Jacques Mallac's account of Claude Peuthé's ascent in 1790.

9 — **Vallée des Prêtres** - Le Peter Both

It was in this valley, donated to the parish of St Louis, that Jacques-Henri Bernardin de Saint-Pierre set one of the scenes from his novel *Paul et Virginie*.

La montagne du Peterboth
The Peterboth mountain

Cliché Gentil

The first photographs of the ascent of Pieter Both date back to 1864. In 1885, a group of mountaineers decided to set iron pegs into the rock in order to make the climb easier. In the 1970s, the Special Mobile Force (SMF) of the Mauritian police replaced these rusty 1885 spikes with stainless steel ones.

171

On 1 January 1971, a group of youths decided to mark the New Year by climbing Pieter Both. A violent thunderstorm ensued. Some members of the group were struck by lightning and suffered serious injuries. One of them, Kadress Chengapen, was knocked off balance and fell into a ravine. The SMF did not recover his body until 5 January.

"La Fenêtre" Plaine Williams. (Port-Louis)

This picture of the Plaines Wilhems region seems to be taken from the top of a mountain, overlooking the Tamarin Falls or the Sept Cascades. From here, one had an impressive view of the west bank of the Black River.

172

Plaines Wilhems

Cliché Gentil.

A hut with a straw roof in the Plaines Wilhems region. The height of the roof indicates the owner's level of affluence. At the beginning of French colonization the inhabitants used the large leaves from the Latan palm tree to cover their huts. The development of the sugar industry in the 19th century led to the use of straw from sugar cane. However, nothing beats vetiver grass.

Plaine Wilhems - Un Troupeau de Cerfs

A herd of deer in Plaines Wilhems. Deer become domesticated easily if given shelter, water, food and lots of space. During the mating season they are more aggressive and can attack people.

Paysage, Pointe aux sables
Landscape, Sandy Point

Cliché Gentil

The coastal resort of Pointe aux Sables is very popular because of its proximity to Port Louis, as well as to the towns of Basses Plaines Wilhems.

Before cars arrived on the island after World War I, the railway network was of paramount importance.

174

A labyrinth of paths and cart tracks wove their way between the railway stations and the sugar factories. These were the precursors to the current road network.

VACOAS. – Usine de Canne à Sucre

A. Rambert - Cliché réservé

The Réunion S.E. sugar factory was built at Beaumanoir in Plaines Wilhems. A Madagascan, Princess Béti, bought it from Monsieur Trébon in 1792. The estate covers almost 160 hectares, with the Rivière du Rempart bordering its western edge. Princess Béti lived here until her death in 1805. However, Curepipe, Vacoas and Quatre Bornes threatened the territorial integrity of Réunion S.E. The sugar factory ceased production in 1980 and a textile factory and shopping centre took its place.

175

5 – Vacoas - Panorama de Mangalkhan

The Mangalkhan racecourse at Floréal bore the mark of the Mauritius Jockey Club. The aim was to establish an alternative racecourse to the one at the Champ de Mars, created and managed since 1812 by the Turf Club in Port Louis. The Jockey Club acquired the grounds at Mangalkhan, and organised their first races on 6 January 1906.

CUREPIPE. - Champ du courses de Mangalkan

C. Vidal - Reproduction Interdite

The Mauritius Jockey Club established the racetrack on land owned by the Gujadhur family. In 1936, the Jockey Club replaced the straw-thatched stands with concrete structures, which are still standing today. The railway line was extended from Floréal to Mangalkhan.

Les courses à Mangalkhan Vacoa.
The Races at Mangalkhan Vacoa.

Cliché Gentil.

By 1954, the Turf Club in Port Louis was so popular and well frequented that there was little interest in organizing race events at Floréal. The riding club at Floréal was established in the 1950s and became the only equestrian activity in the region.

Yacoas. Mauritius Jockey Club.

In 1943, the military requisitioned the Jockey Club stands for offices and accommodation. After World War II, the Health Department converted them into an orthopaedic hospital, during a severe polio epidemic.

7 — Vacoas - Hippodrome - Vue des Loges

After the devastating hurricanes of 1960 and 1961, the government again requisitioned the stands of the Jockey Club as shelter for homeless families. The Floréal racecourse became home to the Residential City of Mangalkhan, made up of public housing. The stands were converted into clinics, social centres, offices and youth clubs.

56. ~ Vacoas. ~ Tribunes de The Mauritius Jockey Club

The Turf Club celebrated its bicentennial in 2012. For over 20 years, there has been talk of building a modern racecourse in another location. Other towns outside of Port Louis have been suggested, such as Guibies at Pailles, La Vigie at Forest Side, Curepipe, Bagatelle, Moka, Médine and Pierrefonds. For the moment, the horse-racing tradition still carries on at the Champ de Mars.

35   Temple Hindou (Vacoas)   Edition des Maga
Reproduction

MAURITIUS
POSTAGE
5c

The Hindu temple at Caverne, Vacoas, is one of the oldest Hindu places of worship in Plaines Wilhems. From the end of the 19th century, it has been used as a resting place for Maha Shivaratri pilgrims heading for the Grand Bassin where they collected holy water to offer to the Hindu deity as a sign of gratitude. Maha Shivaratri, or "the night of Shiva", is an annual festival devoted to Lord Shiva.

QUATRE-BORNES. - Montagne du Corps de Garde

Corps de Garde Mountain separates the towns of Quatre Bornes and Rose Hill from the La Ferme Reservoir, located on the floor of its western valley.

Montagne du Corps de Garde
Corps de Garde Mountain

A view of Corps de Garde Mountain.

Plaine Wilhems — Montagne du Corps de Garde

According to the Littré dictionary a "corps de garde" is a military force that guards the location where it is assigned. Some say that this mountain got its name because its outline resembles a watchdog.

16. MAURITIUS. Séminaire Père Laval — Père Laval's Seminary "Q. Bornes".
"Quatre Bornes".

Édition J. Grancourt et Cie - Tous droits réservés.

The Collège du Saint-Esprit at Quatre Bornes was founded by the seventh bishop of Port Louis, Bishop John Baptist Tuohill Murphy. Due to a lack of funds, the bishop decided to do without an architect, or even blueprints. He was reprimanded because he did not have a building permit.

The former Séminaire Père Laval. This school was renamed Collège du Saint-Esprit in 1938.

This postcard shows the backyard of the Collège du Saint-Esprit, with the assembly hall which served as a gymnasium and the two-storeyed building housing the classrooms.

In 1886, the villages of Beau Bassin and Rose Hill were combined by the government to be managed by a single town council. In 1927, the council decided that they needed a town hall. Victor Singery suggested the local theatre. In the end an architectural competition was held to find a solution. It was Coulhac-Mazérieux's design that won. It envisaged three main buildings, separate but interconnected.

The Anglican St Thomas Church at Beau Bassin. In 1885, Reverend A. Denny, Chief Civil Chaplain of Mauritius, appealed for funds to build new Anglican churches at Beau Bassin (St Thomas) and Réduit (St John). On 10 July 1850, Bishop James Chapman of Colombo consecrated the new St Thomas Church, and two days later St John Church.

Mauritius. „Rose Hill' village (near Railway gate).

Ceci donne une idée exacte de nos pauvres petits villages de campagne

A road in the "village" of Rose Hill near the train station. In the 19th century Port Louis was the only town in Mauritius. It was only around 1890 that places such as Curepipe, Rose Hill and Quatre Bornes formed town councils for better management and hence received the status of "town". Even so, after that these new towns remained for a long time dormitory, i.e. primarily residential, towns.

Rose Hill. La sortie du meeting de Mérandon.

People leaving after a meeting headed by René Mérandon. At the beginning of the 20th century, the economic situation was gloomy and farmers demanded financial support. The order came from London to make an official inquiry into the matter. On 1 June 1908, René Mérandon and Willie Dowson began a tour of the island on a "Caravan of Truth" – a cart pulled by two oxen – to campaign in favour of the Royal Commission.

17 — Digue de Beau-Séjour (Rose-Hill)

Edition des Maga
Reproduction

The Beau-Séjour dam was probably built to retain the waters of the Plaines Wilhems River, and to regulate water flowing into the two channels criss-crossing the region – the Terre Rouge and the Plaines Wilhems.

184

"FANTAISIE"   Beau-Bassin, Ile Maurice

"Fantaisie" estate at Beau Bassin. This town is also famous for its lovely lake at Barkly and the waterfall in Balfour Gardens.

Mauritius. Barkly Asylum, Beau Bassin.

Barkly Asylum, Beau Bassin, c 1905. It was named after Sir Henry Barkly, governor of Mauritius from 1863 to 1870. In the beginning, this asylum took care of the mentally ill as well as the poor and orphaned. The property produced its own fruits and vegetables for the residents. The town was probably named after the beautiful lake found on the grounds. Today, it has become a garden nursery.

14. MAURITIUS. Église de N.-D. de Lourdes. — "N.-D. de Lourdes" Church. Rose Hill.

Édition J. Grancourt et Cie - Tous droits réservés.

The parish church of Notre Dame de Lourdes, Rose Hill.

Petite Rivière — La Fenêtre

"La Fenêtre" is not found at Petite Rivière, but it does offer a breathtaking view of La Ferme Reservoir, with a waterfall over 120 metres high. Beyond this waterfall stretches a reservoir of almost 273 hectares. A stone dam, 1.7 kilometres long, blocks off the western end of this reservoir. This was built between 1913 and 1921 by Englishman M. Harriott, an expert in irrigation.

9 — Phare de la Pointe aux Caves (Petite Rivière)

Edition des Magasins Réunis
Reproduction interdite

The inauguration of Albion Lighthouse took place on 1 October 1910. Lighthouses lost their strategic importance with the advent of radar and satellite observation posts. The Albion Lighthouse, however, remained active. Its counterparts at Gunners' Point and l'île aux Fouquets are, on the other hand, decommissioned.

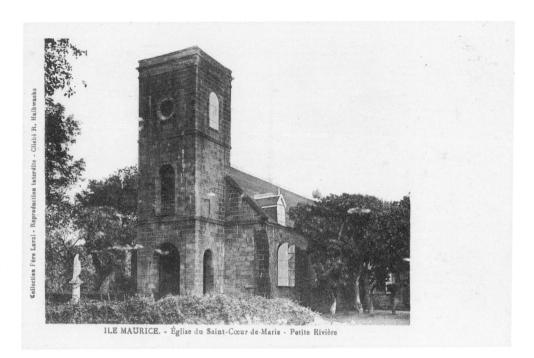

Collection Père Laval - Reproduction interdite - Cliché R. Halbwachs

ILE MAURICE. - Église du Saint-Cœur-de-Marie - Petite Rivière

The church of St Cœur de Marie at Petite Rivière was the first chapel established by Father Laval. In 1847, Ms Desfossés decided to devote herself to converting her neighbours. Her meetings took place in her father's bakery: the entrance to the oven provided a perfect place to display a statue of the Virgin Mary. These new converts decided to build the church of St Cœur de Marie. Romanesque in style, it was built between 1857 and 1861.

187

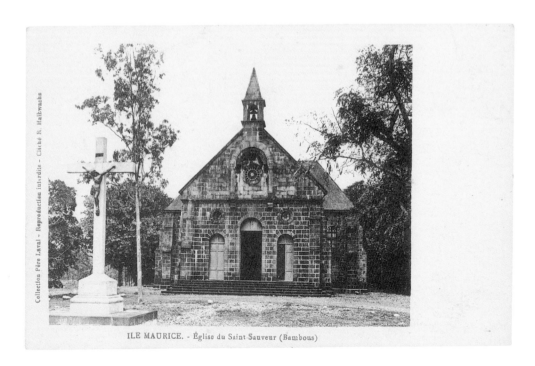

Collection Père Laval - Reproduction interdite - Cliché R. Halbwachs

ILE MAURICE. - Église du Saint-Sauveur (Bambous)

The history of Eglise St Saveur Bambous and that of the neighbouring St Cœur de Marie at Petite Rivière are very similar. In 1846, Father Laval converted a resident of Bambous, who turned his home into a place of worship. A dedicated chapel was much needed and was eventually built upon a quarter-hectare piece of land offered by a convert. Eglise St Saveur was unfortunately destroyed by a cyclone on 8 March 1848. Two landowners then put up the money to build a new and bigger church, and work began in February 1871.

A. Appavou.   96. **Mauritius.**   Flic en Flacq.   Digging for the hidden treasure.

The sender of this postcard (c 1907) wrote on the back in English, "About a century ago, after having anchored at Flic en Flac, the corsairs went down to the village where they hid their booty (a treasure of substantial amount). Some, in possession of so-called treasure maps, began to search for this treasure. Their hunt began in 1901, six years ago. I regret to say that they haven't had any luck so far."

1 — **Flic en Flacq** - La Baie du Corsaire

Treasure hunters cropped up from time to time in the history of Mauritius. They reckoned that pirates would not store their loot on board their ships, for fear of shipwreck or capture by a more powerful enemy. They thought that pirates would instead hide their treasure on shore, the exact spot being known to only a privileged few, or marked on a map.

Flic-en-flac — Bassin Loulou

The Loulou Pond at Flic en Flac, c 1905. On the west coast, in the Black River district, dotted with hotels today, lies the village of Flic en Flac. The name, given by the Dutch, appears to be a distortion of *fried landt flaak*, which can be literally translated as "free flat land".

51. - Montagne des Trois Mamelles

The Trois Mamelles, with the parapet of the Floréal hairpin bend in the foreground and a section of the railway connecting Curepipe and Vacoas on the right. The sugar route, Swami Sivananda Avenue, has replaced the ancient railway.

SOUTH

The south of Mauritius is relatively undeveloped, and features the wildest landscapes. There are at least three main zones: the highlands, the lowlands extending to the basalt cliffs, and a central region separating them at the foot of the Grand Port mountain range.

The Black River district, in the southwest of the island, is the third largest district in Mauritius by area, and the driest. It offers beautiful walks for hikers along a strip of land, sometimes narrow and sparse, wedged between the mountains and the sea. Tagged on to its southern tip is the Savanne district, the most scenic part of the island boasting a wild, rugged coastline. From Pierrefonds to Souillac, motorists take the road that runs for about 50 kilometres following the Black River mountain range. Its craggy peaks are more impressive than the smaller hills in Savanne, but along the shore which, according to poet Paul-Jean Toulet, is where "the soul is born", the natural splendour of crashing waves and rock-strewn coves is undoubtedly the most beautiful on the island. It is difficult to say whether it is the sapphire ocean that accentuates the snowy whiteness of the coastal breakers of Savanne, or if it is the white waves that highlights the intensity of the blue as dark as night.

At Souillac, the mountains fade away into the distance. Cross the sugar cane plains of the Savanne lowlands and other wondrous sights are in store along a belt running between the lagoon and mountains from Mahébourg and up the Grande Rivière Sud-Est.

This pleasant walk can be done in both directions, with great scenery in either case. It is advisable to take into account the position of the sun so that it is not directly in one's face. It is better to journey westwards before noon, and eastwards in the afternoon. There is, however, one exception – the sunset. Yet beware: fifteen minutes before the sun sets, the day will appear as if it will never end. Fifteen minutes later, however, darkness envelops the island and it will be difficult to find one's way through the villages.

From Pierrefonds to Souillac, one will first pass the Corps de Garde on his right, which does not look its best from this angle. The best view of the mountain should be seen from either Quatre Bornes, from the roof of the Collège du Saint-Esprit, or Chebel, where the Corps de Garde mimics the Hauts de Hurlevent. On the left, there is a panoramic view of Trois Mamelles, which is especially beautiful at sunrise.

The quirky peaks of the Montagne du Rempart are best admired from Yémen. The cone-shaped Tourelle du Tamarin is unmistakeable, like the other Black River mountains, including the Piton de la Rivière Noire, the highest point of Mauritius. A detour to the left, at the southern exit of the village of Black River, takes you on a foray into the semi-native forest in the Black River Gorges, home to plant species that grow amazingly tall. Sitting at the bottom of a ravine with steep slopes, they need to grow high to reach the few rays of sunshine available. Hurricane gusts are not a threat because the surrounding cliffs provide protection from winds. Roots grow deep into the basalt ground where soil covering is scarce. Under the tree canopy lurks a moody atmosphere of permanent darkness.

Mahébourg. Barrachois de la Rivière La Chaux.

MAHÉBOURG - Notre-Dame

TOP: Mahébourg, the *barachois* or shallow lagoon of La Chaux River.

ABOVE: The ancient church of Notre Dame des Anges in Mahébourg.

Savane

Port de Souillac

Cascade de Tamarin
Tamarind falls

Cliché Gentil

TOP: Boats on the Savanne River at Souillac, in the period when coastal boats still carried sugar to Port Louis, and returned with merchandise bought in the capital.

ABOVE: One of the waterfalls of Tamarind Falls, a gorge weaving its way through the highlands, before reaching the plains and hunting grounds of Yémen.

From Case Noyale (or Case Royale, as some people say), one can choose to climb either Chamarel or Le Morne Brabant. Steep roads snake up from sea level to Chamarel, at an altitude of 500 metres. There, the splendid view overlooking the coast between Black River and Le Morne, and Île aux Bénitiers, spreads at one's feet. Case Noyale, once a forgotten village but now resurrected by tourism, is charming. Renowned as the capital of African folklore in Mauritius, it draws crowds who come to enjoy the magnificent view of the Baie du Cap. And finally, Le Morne, notorious as a refuge for runaway slaves, was declared a World Heritage Site by UNESCO in 2008.

Between Le Morne and Souillac, the coastal and mountain scenery is beautiful and varied. The unspoilt breathtaking landscape disappears over the cliffs and drops into a calm, but sometimes capricious, ocean. The Baie du Cap looks like a Norwegian fjord. It is sometimes referred to as "de Cap", after an officer on board the *Duc d'Anjou*, a ship of the French East India Company, who in 1736 captured two fugitive slaves aboard a drifting canoe, likely stolen from around Morne Brabant.

The Rocher de Macondé, which once blocked access to the eastern side of the Baie du Cap, now provides a thrilling drive along a road that twists around the giant rock standing in the swirling currents of the deep sea. Macondé, some believe, is named after a Malagasy slave; others say it is named after Jean-Baptiste Henri de Condé, colonel of the Cambrésis regiment.

According to Antoine Chelin, Governor Antoine Marie Desforges-Boucher (1759–1767) asked Henry de Condé to develop an early-warning system on the island to alert the governor in case of an emergency.

For tired drivers, Bel Ombre provides a convenient stop between Souillac and Le Morne Brabant. With Rochester Waterfall, its marine cemetery, Telfair Gardens, the ancient port, the 19th-century police station, and the Gris Gris cliffs, Souillac deserves more than just a a brief stopover. Let your imagination run wild where poets Paul-Jean Toulet, Robert Edward Hart, Sophia, Harilal R. Vaghjee, Maurice Rault and Max Moutia were once inspired; or just sit back and listen to the hum of casuarina trees caressing the winds and the waves.

Between Souillac and Mahébourg, there is no lack of interesting sights: the restaurant and rum distillery in St Aubin, La Vanille Réserve with its baby crocodiles and tortoises, the natural beauty of Andréa, Bel Air, Bénarès, Le Souffleur, Pont Naturel and, finally, the centuries-old charm of Mahébourg. Then, the road veers off again, for 25 kilometres, between the mountain and the sea.

The Montagne du Lion, or rather Lions, is the only mountain in Grand Port of any interest. From the airport or Pointe des Régates in Mahébourg, a vigilant peak stares west under the admiring gaze of the visitor. Fifty to a hundred metres after the police station at Bois des Amourettes, we stumble across another lion-shaped peak, asleep this time, the muzzle pointing north. A little further north, a short steep walk from the coast road provides breathtaking views from the Pointe du Diable over the lagoon. The devil that guards its treasure here is said to be responsible for the bizarre compass readings on vessels approaching this point. Also here are fortifications, the finest in Mauritius, that were built by the French in the 18th century. The coast road continues north hugging the sea, until it reaches the Grande Rivière Sud-Est.

The bridge used by the trams of the St Marie sugar factory. This factory, situated at the mouth of the Baie du Jacotet, was the scene of a British invasion in May 1810.

Pointe aux Roches is situated at the western end of the Pomponnette public beach. From this spot one can admire the South Pole swells that crash down on this coastal basaltic plateau.

41. - Bénarès - Bord de Mer

Bénarès got its name from a sugar cane estate that was active until 1968. In 1859, the politician Sir Virgil Naz acquired Bénarès where he built a palatial summer home. It was demolished in 1937.

Edition des Magasins Réunis
Reproduction interdite

28 — Rade de Mahébourg (Mouchoir Rouge)

The waterfront between the Pointe Canon and the Pointe des Régates is a thriving centre for local fishing and boat races. Traditional flat-bottomed fishing boats, called pirogues, regularly land there. During regattas many pirogues are decorated with colourful sails.

MAHÉBOURG. - Pointe des Régates

E. Vidal - Reproduction interdite

The famous Mahébourg Regatta is greeted with enthusiasm by competitors and the local community. Other coastal villages try to outdo the Mahébourg Regatta, but it still remains the dominant boat race in the region. When a regatta is announced at Mahébourg, Grand Port residents rush to participate, all wanting to maintain the reputation of the eastern coastal villages.

Rade de Mahébourg

The bay of Mahébourg, c 1909. Here, even today, the long, thin racing pirogues jostle side by side with the simple wider-bottomed fishing boats. Two monuments stand at Vieux Grand Port, one commemorating the arrival of the Dutch, the other the introduction of sugar cane.

Vue de la Rade de Mahebourg - Le Mouchoir rouge

The Grand Port Regatta is the boating event of the year for all residents of Mahébourg. The governor, who lives at Château du Réduit, is always eager to join in the festivities. Also keen to participate are the English and Mauritius aristocracy, as well as large crowds of local people.

If, during a regatta, the shore is too crowded, the more adventurous spectator can charter a pirogue to take up prime position out in the bay for the start of the race. This postcard is famous for having served as the model for the cherry-coloured two-cent stamp, belonging to the 1950s Mauritian landscape series.

A view of the island of Mouchoir Rouge from Pointe des Régates.

Mouchoir Rouge faces Mahébourg's waterfront and its bus terminal.

Mauritius. „Mouchoir Rouge" Island Grand Port.

According to legend, the Îlot du Mouchoir Rouge (Red Handkerchief Islet) is so named because when people on it wanted to go to Mahébourg they would wave a red scarf to indicate to the pirogues that they should come and pick them up.

LE MOUCHOIR ROUGE. MAHEBOURG. QUARTIER DU GRAND PORT

Mouchoir Rouge inspired Mauritian landscape painters, such as Xavier Le Juge de Segrais.

MAHÉBOURG. - Mouchoir rouge

E. Vidal - Reproduction interdite

In his book, *Mahébourg, ville virtuelle*, Lilian Berthelot wrote that, around 1860, Henri Edwin Dennie leased Mouchoir Rouge where he built a salt works, a vegetable garden and a bathing area facing the open sea.

There are no restrictions on the colour that Mouchoir Rouge residents may paint their houses; they have chosen vermillion. The same colour has been used for the roof of Notre-Dame Auxiliatrice Chapel, at Cap Malheureux.

Bord de mer Mahébourg.
Sea shore Mahebourg.

Cliché Gentil.

The lagoon at the Mahébourg seafront and the Pointe d'Esny has crystal clear waters.

Mahébourg — Naufrage du « Dalblair » — Pointe d'Esny

On 5 February 1902, the *Dalblair*, while under Captain A. Mentys' command, ran aground on the coral reef off Pointe d'Esny. It was carrying a cargo of coal, which did not go to waste as the local residents salvaged it and used it as fuel in the months after the accident.

Bord de Mer, Mahébourg.
Sea shore at Mahebourg.

Cliché Gentil.

The currents off the coast of Mahébourg prevent the build-up of stagnant water. The beaches have powder-fine white sand.

" Le Souffleur " Souvenir du 8 novembre 1925. (Port-Louis)

Le Souffleur is a cleft in a basaltic cliff. At this spot, in contrast to the calm lagoons, the crashing waves swell into the gap in the rock. As the pressure builds up, the natural blowhole shoots water to heights of up to ten metres, with a deafening roar.

Blue Bay. Grand Port.

Blue Bay stands out for its proximity to a marine park and Deux Cocos Island. A Moorish-style hotel stands here, that once belonged to Governor Hesketh Bell.

Maurice. L'entrée de la gare du chemin de fer. Mahébourg.

A view of the train track leading to Mahébourg Station.

Mahébourg – La Gare

Train travel was expensive in the early 20th century. For example, a one-way ticket from Port Louis to Mahébourg cost 4.32 rupees in first class, 2.88 rupees in second class and 1.44 rupees in third class. A return ticket to the same destination cost 6.48 rupees in first class and 4.32 rupees in second class. To put this into perspective, a farm worker at that time earned less than one rupee a day. Today, a farm worker earns more than 300 times the value of a rupee in 1916.

203

7 – Mahébourg - Central Station

The entrance of Mahébourg Station, c 1906. The station was the terminus of the Centre Line. The station, located to the right of the picture and not visible in this image, was inaugurated in 1865. Travelling from Curepipe and Rose-Belle, the train suddenly burst out onto the coast and ran along the seafront, offering travellers a wonderful view of Grand Port Bay.

At the Pointe des Régates, Mahébourg, stands an obelisk in honour of the French and British who lost their lives during the Grand Port naval battle of August 1810.

Plaisance Airport

In the 1960s, a new terminal welcomed passengers at Plaisance airport. The new building replaced the military bunkers with their black iron roofs. In recent years there has been talk of building a new terminal inspired by the shape of *Ravenala madagascariensis* or the traveller's tree.

The crew of the few aircraft landing at
Mauritius in 1952 stayed at the straw-roofed
Hotel Chaland, one of the first hotels on
the island. In the early 1980s, the Chaland
became the luxurious Shandrani Hotel.

A reception room at the Hotel Chaland.

Cliché G. Rehaut

Débarcadère de MAHEBOURG

Landing place at MAHEBOURG

Mahébourg Jetty is a meeting place for fishermen and *banians* (middlemen). These middlemen provide the capital for the fishermen to buy boats, sails, engines and lockers. In return, the fishermen reserve for them the best of their catch.

MAHÉBOURG. - Marché aux Poissons

E. Vidal - Reproduction interdite

The Fish Market in Mahébourg, c 1909. Fishermen set off in pirogues from all along this coast, to fish in the bay or beyond. In the evening they return with their catch to this open air market.

The estuary of the River La Chaux, the name of which often leads to confusion. For the Dutch, it is the Limoen River or 'River of Lemons', because citrus fruit is planted on its banks. The English correctly translated it as Lime River, while the French translate the English term 'lime' as 'limestone' (chalk or *chaux*).

Mahébourg — Entrée de la Rivière la Chaux

Mahébourg — Pont sur la Rivière la Chaux

The ancient wooden bridge over La Chaux River. The bridge measured 20 metres long, and rose to a height of 3 metres.

39. ~ Mahebourg. ~ Pont de la Rivière La Chaux

This 152-metre-long bridge made of reinforced concrete is named after Governor Cavendish Boyle (1904–1911). Designed by Paul Le Juge de Segrais, it has seven piles, placed at 20-metre intervals. It is the longest bridge in Mauritius, and was built to replace the original wooden bridge, dating from 1850, which could not support the heavy trailers introduced to transport sugar.

11 — Mahébourg - Le Pont Nolino

Cliché G. Déhaut - Noël Grégoire

The Molino Bridge (here incorrectly spelled Nolino) spans the Champagne River. Nearby stand two monuments, one commemorating the arrival of the Dutch in Mauritius, and the other the introduction of sugar cane and the Java deer.

MAHÉBOURG. - Monument élevé à la Mémoire des Héros morts
dans le Combat de l'Ile de la Passe

E. Vidal - Reproduction interdite

A monument erected in memory of the heroes who perished in the battle of Île de la Passe.

38. ~ Mahebourg. - Montagne du Lion

A view of Lion Mountain as seen from Pointe des Régates, Mahébourg.

Usine de Sucre "Mont Désert Carrie". - MAHEBOURG

The Carie Mon Désert sugar factory (named after one of its owners), c 1908. The factory later merged with *Mon Trésor* which had an extensive railway network. Trams circulated throughout the fields and brought sheaves of sugar cane to it.

44. – Le Phare de l'île de la Passe

Île aux Fouquets and Île au Phare are part of the island chain that formed along the coral reef, stretching from Blue Bay to the Grande Rivière Sud-Est, protecting the Grand Port lagoon. These islands, long neglected, have now become popular tourist hotspots.

Maurice. Le Phare de Mahébourg.

5. Église catholique de MAHEBOURG

Romain catholique church of Mahebourg

Cliché G. Behaut

The Mahébourg Lighthouse was built in 1864 on Île aux Fouquets which sits next to Île de la Passe, scene of many bloody conflicts during the famous Battle of Vieux Grand Port between French and English sailors. The name Grand Port is included among the list of battles on the pillars of the Arc de Triomphe in Paris.

The Catholic Church of Mahébourg (c 1909) was a church in one of the five parishes that were created in 1770. The church was built in 1849 on land donated by the Kervern family, who owned land in Grand Port. The building was later enlarged in 1938.

Baie du Cap - Pointe Macondé

MACONDÉ
BAY DU CAP

Rambert- Cliché réservé

MAURICE — Une Cascade

2 CENTS

The setting of the Macondé rock is a mixture of incongruous elements: basalt rock, a nurturing yet ruthless sea, currents both hostile and beneficial to sailors, lava sinking into the ocean, and the half-animal, half-mineral coral reef.

The Chamarel waterfall is named after Toussaint and Charles de Chazal de Chamarel. These two brothers were the first to set up business here, providing timber to the colony. Later, Amédée Perrot built a sugar factory here around 1860.

47. - Souillac. - Le Gris Gris

Swells from the South Pole, sea spray, gusty winds and lashing rains have carved Dantean shapes out of the rock at Gris Gris Beach. People who walk along the sandy beach sometimes come up with names for the formations sculpted by the relentless elements, such as the Witch, Virgin of the Rocks and the Comforter of the Afflicted.

213

Plage au „Grigri", Savanne
Sea shore „The Grigri", Savanne

Cliché Gentil

At the western end of Gris Gris Beach stands a massive rocky outcrop at the foot of the cliff called La Roche qui Pleure (The Crying Rock). It is so named because when the wild sea crashes over the rock it leaves behind a slow-flowing white foam resembling tears.

52. ~ Savane. ~ Allée de Filaos

Mauritius. „Rivière du Porte" Savanne.

An alley of extremely tall casuarina trees on the coast road runs along the valley that borders the Pomponnette public beach. Since this image was taken the road has been reconstructed to allow space for a seafront hotel.

The torrential waters of Rivière du Poste.

Cascade de la Savane

Terracina was a sugar property in the late 18th century, in Savanne district. After World War II, it merged with Compagnie Union. One passes through Terracina to reach this waterfall, known as Rochester Falls, one of the most significant in Mauritius alongside those of Tamarin, Réduit, and Chamarel.

Cascade de Terracine - Savane

A view of Rochester Falls. Rochester is also the name of a sugar factory bought in 1830 by Joseph Chalines, owner of Terracina.

Bain des Négresses. Souillac. Maurice.

Bain des Négresses is the name of a river whose source is near the Bois Chéri tea factory and the Piton Savanne. Bain des Négresses is also the name given to a 330-acre sugar estate owned by Union S.E. between 1871 and 1877.

Savanne. Le Battelage du Petit Cap.

The ancient port of Bel Ombre. Until 1950, ships transported sugar to Port Louis, and returned with various other goods. Guy Rouillard, in his *Histoire des domaines sucriers*, says that the *Jean-Chantal* was the last ship to carry goods from here.

Savanne. Eglise du Petit Cap.

Reverend Lucien Mengelle (of the congregation of St Esprit) was known as the Apostle of the Savanne, and was the reverend for the chapel of St François d'Assise at Baie du Cap. In February 1886, he became priest at Souillac-Chemin-Grenier. His superiors wanted him to succeed Bishop Le Roy, the bishop of Gabon. Mengelle pleaded with them to choose another clergyman and leave him with his Savanne flock.

217

Audusson et Vidal. — Mauritius

Savanne. Baie du Cap

At the Baie du Cap the mountain slopes fall steeply down to the sea. A bridge (not pictured) crosses this inlet.

SAVANNE. - Baie du Cap

A winding road follows the shores of the Savanne bay and channels its way inland, eventually reaching the mouth of the river of the same name.

Baie du Cap

A. Rambert - Cliché réservé

Another view of Baie du Cap.

The Petit-Cap *barachois* ('lagoon' or 'pool' in Creole), at the eastern entrance of the Baie du Cap, is one of the most difficult to access, especially in bad weather.

The Anguilles River rises from the land encircling the Bois Chéri tea factory. It continues in a southwesterly direction towards the villages of Tyack and Rivière des Anguilles.

Maurice. La Pointe Macondée du Petit-Cap. Savanne.

| Macondé Point at Baie du Cap.

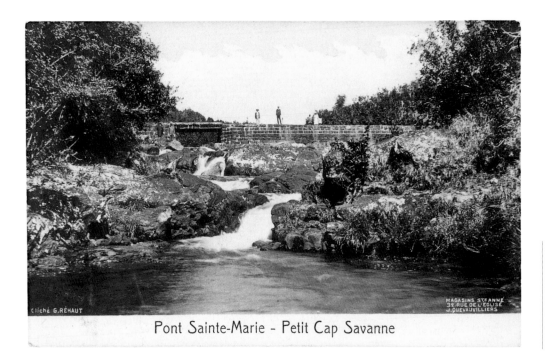

Cliché G.RÉHAUT

MAGASINS Ste ANNÉ
39, RUE DE L'EGLISE
J. QUEVAUVILLIERS

Pont Sainte-Marie - Petit Cap Savanne

The Creole poet Paul-Jean Toulet
(1867–1920) wrote about this part of the
island:
Et toi, Savane en fleurs
Que l'océan trempe de pleurs
Et le soleil de flamme;
Douce aux ramiers, douce aux amants,
Toi de qui la ramure
Nous charmait d'ombre et de murmure,
Et de roucoulements

Pont du Chemin de Fer - Rivière du Poste (Savanne)

Contrary to the caption printed on this postcard, the bridge pictured is the St Marie Bridge at Petit Cap in Savanne, not the railway bridge at Rivière du Poste.

2. Pont de Ste-Marie, petit Cap Savanne
St-Mary's bridge, petit Cap Savanne

Cliché G. Rehaut

This bridge is built on stilts planted in the Creole Creek estuary, at Baie du Cap.

43. ~ Embouchure de la grande rivière Sud Est

The mouth of the Grande Rivière Sud-Est.

AURICE — Cascade de la Grande Rivière

The Grande Rivière Sud-Est, along with Ferney-Vieux Grand Port, Port Louis and the Black River, was one of the first places to be colonized by the Dutch. The estuary of this fast-flowing river has broken through the coral reef, and created what is now the north entrance to the vast Grand Port lagoon.

5 – **Maurice** - Le Bac de Grand-Rivière S. E.

Cliché G. Déhaut - Noël Grégoire

At the other end of the North line, the railway station is found on the left bank of the Grande Rivière Sud-Est. A ferry system was established to bring passengers who lived on the opposite bank to the station.

14 – **Maurice** - La Mairie (le Filtre)

Cliché G. Déhaut - Noël Grégoire

The Mare aux Vacoas is today one of the main reservoirs in Mauritius. The La Marie filtering station treats water taken from the reservoir so that it is suitable for drinking.

35 – La Mare aux Vacoas

On 3 March 1888 a banquet was held at Rose Hill to celebrate the inauguration of a public water system. At the time the water in the Mare aux Vacoas reservoir had a depth of nearly ten metres. The honour of opening the valve was given to Francis Fleming, the interim governor. Mare aux Vacoas first appears on a map in 1722, and was officially acknowledged by cartographer Abbey La Caille in 1753.

4 — Maurice - La Mare aux Vacoas

The families Gassin and Bouloc were the first to stake their claim at Mare Aux Vacoas. The owners Numa and Alexandre Paillotte, Louis Blanchette, Alcide Bonnefin, Eugène Mancel and Albert Lucas built a sugar factory here, which was named Alexandrie after Alexandre Paillotte.

In 1880, Mr Thompson, assistant conservator of forests in India, advised Governor George Bowen to develop the land around Mare aux Vacoas and build a reservoir for domestic drinking water.

Four factors spurred the creation of a reservoir at Mare aux Vacoas: population growth; the construction of two railway lines between 1864 and 1865; the onset of fatal epidemics from 1854; and the steady rise in the standard of living. From 1888 to 1988, the capacity of the Mare aux Vacoas reservoir multiplied by 24 times.

BRIDGE ON THE BLACK RIVER.
VIADUC SUR LA RIVIERE NOIR.   G. MOLLIÈRES. COPYRIGHT

The bridge over the Black River, in the location and district of the same name.

On 13 December 1934, the wife of Governor Wilfrid Jackson inaugurated the new Tamarin Bridge. The floods of December 1929 had carried away the previous bridge, the ruins of which can just been seen to the right of the new one.

15. MAURITIUS. Phare de la "Pointe aux Caves". — "Pointe aux Caves" Light-House.

Edition J. Gtancourt et Cie - Tous droits réservés.

The inauguration of the Pointe aux Caves Lighthouse took place on 1 October 1910. This lighthouse sits atop a tower 65 metres in height.

37. ~ Rivière Noire. - Le Phare de la Pointe aux Caves

In late May 1952, an electric motor replaced the old oil-fired mechanism at the Pointe aux Caves Lighthouse.

42. - Rivière Noire. - Rivière des Galets

Galets River in Mauritius flows through the Savanne district, and not the Black River district. It rises from the Mares region, on the Champagne Plains, tumbles down a 500-foot waterfall, crosses the Valriche region, and then flows towards the towns of Chamouny and Chemin-Grenier.

33 - Baie du Tamarin. - Montagne du Rempart

As the crow flies, there is only six kilometres between the jagged peak of the Montagne du Rempart and the estuaries of the rivers Bucan, Tamarin and Rempart.

A view of the opposite face of the Trois Mamelles, also known as the Montagne du Rempart. On 29 April 1982, 200 people died at the Beau Bassin sugar factory when it was destroyed by a violent cyclone.

Montagne des trois Mamelles, Usine à sucre "Bassin„ - Rivière noire.
The "Trois Mamelles" Mountain, The sugar estate "Bassin" Rivière-noire.   Cliché Gentil.

The Morne Brabant. This outcrop of basaltic rock, rising to a height of 243 metres, has a vertical cliff face so steep that it is almost impossible to climb to the summit. The Morne Brabant is a designated UNESCO World Heritage Site.

34. ~ Rivière Noire ~ Le Morne

Souillac port, c 1909. Situated on the south coast, the port provided natural shelter for vessels that transported sacks of sugar to Port Louis, and brought goods back from the capital. In 1878, the railway was introduced. The train was more reliable and less dangerous than coastal shipping. In 1964, the automobile replaced the train.

230

The former railway station at Souillac was one of the few red brick buildings built in Mauritius in the 19th century. Along with the police station (an 18th-century former French military post built from stone), the washhouse and the Telfair Gardens, it adds a certain charm to the village.

48. ~ Souillac. ~ Le Havre

To the right of Souillac Wharf stands the town's marine cemetery. The famous historian, archivist and statistician D'Unienville, poets Robert Edward Hart and Maurice Rault, and scientist Robert Antoine are among the illustrious people buried here.

231

A. Appavou.   46. Mauritius. Bay of Souillac.

Viscount François de Souillac, governor of Mauritius from May 1779 to April 1785, created the district of Savanne in 1787. He was charged with making the inlet more practicable; Port Souillac was named in honour of the Viscount's contribution to the development of the town.

45. ~ L'Ile de la Passe

Île de la Passe, with its ancient fortifications, guards the south entry to Grand Port.

46. ~ L'Ile de la Passe. ~ Vieilles Fortifications

In the 18th century, the French built defences on the Île de la Passe. These fortifications included ramparts, artillery batteries, gunpowder magazines, hot-shot furnaces, barracks, water tanks, lookout posts and signal masts. However, none of this prevented the British from capturing the island by surprise on the night of 18 August 1810. Île de la Passe also formed part of the integrated defence of southern Mauritius during World War II.

36 ~ Les Sept Cascades

The Sept Cascades, c 1908. The engineer Fanucci harnessed the force of these stunning waterfalls to fuel the first hydroelectric plant in Mauritius. The Mauritian General Electric Supply Company later established a power grid throughout the island.

Cascade de Tamarin
Tamarind falls

The obstacle-ridden, raging Sept Cascades, also known as Tamarind Falls, is a popular location for high-adrenalin sports, such as canyoning.

THE PEOPLE
OF MAURITIUS

In the 1960s, the Soviet Union, flaunting its supposed anti-imperialist principles, insisted that the British Empire abolish colonization, and hand back the colonies to their original populations. One day, at a session of the United Nations, a British delegate asked his Soviet counterparts if, in the Mauritian case, they were alluding to the dodo, an animal which became extinct after the first settlers arrived on the island. It is true that Mauritius, like the other islands of the Mascarenhas Archipelago – Réunion and Rodrigues, along with the Chagos Archipelago and the Seychelles – had never had an indigenous population, or even permanent residents.

The first human settlers were the Dutch who arrived in 1638, and the island was not, strictly speaking, colonized. In fact, the few hundred Dutch who settled here eventually abandoned the island on 17 February 1710, and it was not until 24 December 1721 that the first French settlers arrived – sixteen residents from the neighbouring island of Bourbon (Réunion) – and renamed the island Île de France. However, they did not come to a deserted island: we know that the German Wilhelm Leichnig had settled at the foot of a waterfall in the Beau Bassin district – Plaines Wilhems (the central district of the highlands) was named after him. After the departure of the Dutch, there were probably fugitive slaves who lived on Mauritius as well. They would have had time to explore the island and set up home in the more temperate inland regions, but they would not have been able to stop the French from doing the same.

The first French colonists – who came mainly from Brittany and Normandy, but also from the mountainous regions of Savoy and Franche Comté – came up against the same difficulties as their predecessors. They failed in their attempts to develop the colony, hampered by a hostile tropical climate and the lack of a strategic plan or command structure.

The situation changed radically with the arrival of Governor Mahé de La Bourdonnais on 4 June 1735. His aim was to make Port Louis a naval base capable of meeting the needs of French ships sailing to and from India. Everything Île de France lacked, he brought over from neighbouring Île Bourbon: labour, tools, carts and pack animals. Before his departure on 6 April 1747, he directed the efforts to transform the shanty town into a port town, with naval workshops and shipyards. To fulfil his massive labour needs, a large number of slaves were imported, as well as Tamil craftsmen, shipwrights and Muslim sailors, commonly known as *lascars*.

On 12 October 1725, the French government conducted the first census of Île de France. A total of 213 residents were counted, comprising 20 officers and employees, 100 soldiers, 28 workers, five servants, 13 women, 13 children, 24 slaves belonging to the French East India Company and 10 privately owned slaves. The census of 24 November 1729 listed 486 non-Europeans, including 178 from New Guinea and 89 soldiers. By the time La Bourdonnais landed on the island, Port Louis had 1,676 inhabitants, and Port Bourbon (Grand Port) 246. The census of 28 November 1776 registered 6,386 Europeans, 25,154 slaves and 1,199 free non-Europeans,

ABOVE: The altar of St Sacrament, during the Feast of Corpus Christi.

NEXT PAGE: In 1843, Alexandre Dumas published *Georges*, which was set in Mauritius. Race and racism are at the centre of this novel, which tells of the rise, through the social hierarchy, of a charismatic leader of the black population who clung fiercely to his hatred of the white Franco-Mauritian oligarchy. This novel, written with the help of archivists familiar with Mauritius, is a literary picture of the island before 1835; that is, before the abolition of slavery. A chapter is dedicated to the Festival of Yamsé, or Ghoons, which is depicted on both of these postcards.

YAMSÉ. – Danse des Tigres

YAMSÉ. – Le Ghoon

OPPOSITE: In *Georges*, Alexandre Dumas writes that the Muslim festival of Yamsé is a "symbolic gymnastics" consisting of races, dancing, and fighting accompanied by music and singing. Some participants carry replicas of tombs (or ghoons) on their heads. Others are armed with swords or scimitars, and whirl around the ghoons miming a mock sword battle. Others beat their chests, and roll around on the floor shouting, "Yamsay! Yamli! O Ali!" The next day, there is a procession of ghoons even taller than those of the previous day. They are decorated with coloured paper and lit with lanterns. It takes several men to carry them. The crowd chants melancholic songs. The torchbearers precede the ghoons; the dance of the ghoons and the mock sword fighting begins again in an even wilder frenzy.

making a total of 32,739 inhabitants on the island. This number grew further from 40,439 in 1787 to 59,020 in 1797, and then from 77,768 in 1807 to 96,945 in 1830 (under British rule). Just before the abolition of slavery on 1 February 1835, the number of slaves was estimated to be at least 70,000 – even though slavery had been illegal since 14 January 1813.

The slaves came from different African countries and Madagascar, spoke different languages, and had different customs and cultural backgrounds. Once in Mauritius, the slave traders bundled them together arbitrarily, but the slaves responded by inventing a common language, Creole, which still creates a bond amongst Mauritians today. Mass immigration, and successive waves of thousands of indentured Indian labourers sent to work in the sugar industry, even before the abolition of slavery, changed the social and demographic balance of the island. The Mauritian population grew from 158,432 inhabitants in 1846 to 310,050 in 1861, and then to 370,588 in 1891.

At that time seven out of 10 Mauritians came from India, notably Bihar. They had several things in common: language (Bhojpuri, Hindi, Tamil, Telugu, Marathi, Urdu), religion (Islam and Hindu, which grew extensively in Mauritius) and expertise (in the cultivation of sugar cane). Each encampment became a mini India, giving rise to a vast market and attracting more affluent Indians. The first Indian fortunes in Mauritius were made in the sugar cane fields, but not without hardship. In October 1901, these new entrepreneurs were encouraged by Gandhi's representative to Mauritius, Manilal Doctor, and the first Hindu missionaries of the reformist Arya Samaj movement to invest in the education of their most promising children. In the early 20th century, the first university graduates of Indian descent took their place, with ease, in Mauritian society.

Some Indians set up businesses, trading in jewellery, canvas, grain, cereals, rice, cooking oil and spices. Muslim merchants developed trade in the region; their business contacts, who were often relatives, were established in all the major ports in the western Indian Ocean (Réunion, Madagascar, the Comoros, south and east Africa, the Persian Gulf, Bombay and, of course, their native Gujarat).

During the second half of the 19th century, waves of immigrants from China, fleeing famine, settled in Mauritius. The social organization, or captaincy, of these Chinese immigrants was very important. The leaders, referred to as captains, acted as heads of the community and represented the Chinese authorities in Mauritius. They also acted as the spokesperson and intermediary between their countrymen and the colonial government.

A typical immigrant would take up an apprenticeship at a major Chinese merchant at Port Louis, and when the owner considered that he was ready, would open up his own business in a rural region that did not yet have a Chinese shop. Once his fortune had been made in the countryside, he could re-establish himself in town. The merchants in the rural areas would come to Port Louis once a week to replenish their stocks, pay their debts and exchange valuable information with other clan members, especially news about future political events. They would report back to the captain any news that they had discreetly picked up, or overheard from their clients' conversations in the countryside. The most adept would be sent as reinforcements to other outlets established in the southwest part of the Indian Ocean. Others would be sent back to China to strengthen family ties, establish new business contacts and negotiate with new partners, especially at Guangzhou (then Canton) and Hong Kong, the two principal shipping ports. Cognisant of their small numbers, Chinese shopkeepers traded with Mauritian customers from all ethnic, cultural and religious backgrounds without discrimination, whereas their European, Hindu or Muslim counterparts preferred doing business, almost exclusively, with their own countrymen.

After the travails of the two World Wars, the crash of 1929 and the Great Depression, the new non-European elite, including the first local professionals and university graduates, slowly came into their own. At the same time, the militancy of the working class stepped up within the first trades unions in Mauritius.

After World War II, change came rapidly. It was impossible to hold back the nationalist movement, which strode forward, almost entirely without violence, to develop a ministerial system (in 1957), universal adult suffrage (1959), self-government (1963) and political independence (1968), finally culminating in the Republic of Mauritius (1992).

It is difficult, of course, in the early 21st century to find remnants of the early immigrants' original cultures. However, there is not a single Mauritian who cannot recount the personal story of his ancestors in the history of Mauritius. Mauritians are united by the realization that they are all descendants of immigrants, and are proud of it, proud of what they managed to achieve on these islands where the ships of their ancestors once dropped anchor.

„Les Ghoons", fête religieuse indienne
Indian religious festival

Cliché Gentil

Vue générale des Fêtes de Ghoons
et des Jamsés, Belle-Vue (Mapou)

Indian Festival (Ghoons) on Belle-Vue
Estate Mapou

The Great Ghoon was supposed to represent Karbala, the village where Hussein died, as well as his tomb. Bare-bodied men painted their bodies to look like tigers or the miraculous lion that watched over the remains of the holy preacher. During the procession, these men would roar and leap to scare the crowds.

The rivers of Mauritius were used as public washing places. The washerwomen soaked their laundry in the river, scrubbed it with soap, and then rinsed it in the water. They then took the washing and thrashed it against the rocks several times to rid it of excess water. Mark Twain, during his stay in Mauritius in April 1896, devotes a few lines to the washerwomen, who tried to "split [these basaltic rocks] in two".

Fête Indienne „Ghoon"
Indian Festival „Ghoon"

Cliché Gentil

The feast of Yamsé draws to an end. The devotees must destroy and bury the ghoons. When midnight struck, the torchbearers approached and set fire to the four corners of the ghoons. They then rushed forward to throw them into the river.

Stalks of sugar cane over 4 metres high. The mountain in the background could be the Corps de Garde, as seen from Albion, Petite Rivière, or La Tourelle de Tamarin.

A. Appavou. 99. **Mauritius.** Creole-Malgache Women.

60. ~ Type de Créole

A postcard showing a family of
Madagascan origin. The clothes indicate a
certain affluence – wearing a headscarf or
putting on a cloak or cape is considered
formal dress.

The cap, the jacket and the belt indicate
that this man has taken great care in his
attire. But his shoes are missing.

Type d'Indien

59. – Type d'Indien

241

Poverty is more visible here. However, wearing a jacket over the *langouti* (an Indian garment) adds a touch of elegance.

Improvisation is also more common here. With rations of rice and dried grain balanced on his head and the tent under his arm, this man is still not too weighed down to pose for a picture.

Nain de 18 ans
Dwarf 18 years old

Cliché Gentil

Great respect is given to dwarves in Mauritius, as well as special protection by family and neighbours, since they are believed to bring good luck.

An elderly couple. The way the shawl is worn, like a Madagascan *lamba*, means that they are likely to be of Madagascan origin.

243

A man standing in front of a ravenala (or traveller's palm). This tree can grow up to 20 metres tall, and has large fan-like leaves that collect rainwater. Guy Rouillard and Joseph Guého believe that Princess Béty, of royal Madagascan blood, was the first to introduce the tree into Mauritius in the 18th century.

Vanilla cultivation in Mauritius.

Coconut trees and native huts, c 1909.

Mother and daughter standing in front of a
humble dwelling.

Ile Maurice. – Au Bouchon visite chez une paroissienne
agée de 115 ans

Ile Maurice – Missionnaire Belge entouré de païens.

Depending on the publication date of
these two postcards – before or after 1910
– it can be assumed that this Belgian
missionary was attached either to the
Catholic parish of Mahébourg, or that of
New Grove.

In 1910, the diocese of Port Louis
established the parishes of Mahébourg and
New Grove.

CUREPIPE. - Case d'Indiens

E. Vidal - Reproduction interdite

An Indian hut in Curepipe in the early 20th century.

A family of Indian descent. The Hindu saris resemble the Muslim veil, whereas the boy is wearing a *langouti*, typically a Hindu garment.

E. Vidal - Reproduction interdite

77. - CUREPIPE. - Danse de Singe

A circus monkey trained to perform many tricks.

E. Vidal - Reproduction interdite

76. - CUREPIPE. - Singe savant

Such entertainment was very popular, and hence could be very profitable for the monkey trainer.

CUREPIPE. - Chasse aux Cerfs

A. Rambert - Cliché réservé

A hunting party after a deer shoot. The deer, in particular the Javan rusa, was first introduced to Mauritius in 1639. These hunting expeditions helped regulate the number of deer on the island.

78. - ILE MAURICE. Rabatteurs Indigènes

E. Vidal, Reproduction interdite

The beaters were essential for any deer hunt. They were posted at strategic spots and would drive the deer in front of the hunters by shouting loudly: "Hoo la! Hoo la!"

Un Samedi de courses à Port-Louis
The Saturday's Races, Port-Louis

A race day at the Champ de Mars
racecourse in Port Louis.

Famille d'Indiens

A Mauritian family of Indian origin. The hut's roof is made using vetiver grass, which is of a better quality than sugar cane straw. The men were wearing jackets, which indicate a degree of affluence.

Another family of Indian origin, evident from the saris the women are wearing. Here, the walls are made of stone, and glass protects the porch from bad weather.

58. ~ Femmes Indiennes

A group of Indian women gathered in front of an administrative office.

The fez worn by some people on this postcard indicates that they were probably celebrating the Muslim festival of Yamsé, or Ghoon.

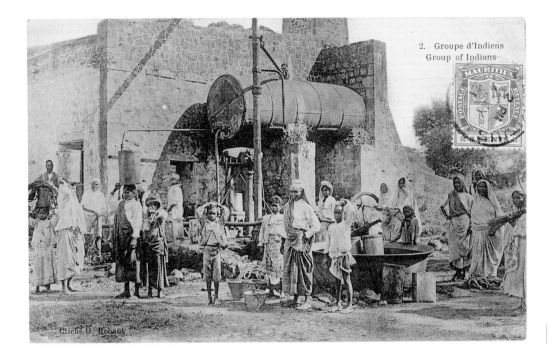

Mauritians of Indian origin assembled in front of a sugar factory.

At Tamarind Falls the living conditions were more difficult. The thatch covering the roof, for example, is in bad repair.

The living conditions were even worse here. The roof, made of sugar cane straw, indicates limited means. Walking to and from the hut in the dark would be dangerous due to the rocky terrain.

Crossing the estuary of the Grande Rivière Sud-Est on a ferry, which was later replaced by a simple pirogue. A bridge located about a kilometre upstream allows motorists to cross the estuary more conveniently.

57. ~ Gâteaux Indiens

Indian delicacies (*moutayes*) piled up for sale in pyramidal or cylindrical forms.

The main courtyard of the town hall in Rose Hill was used as a common square for holding major public events such as concerts, recitals, sports competitions and political meetings.

The Pleasure Ground at Port Louis at the beginning of the 20th century, which later became known as the Robert Edward Hart Gardens, after the Mauritian poet. The crowds gathered here could be enjoying the festivities before the coronation of George V.

255

On 1 June 1908, Willie Dowson and René Mérandon left Port Louis on their wagon "Truth on the March", campaigning in support of the upcoming royal commission. It was hoped that this report would secure British financial support for Mauritius.

Inauguration du Buste de Remy Ollier
21 Novembre 1908

Inauguration of the Bust of Remy Ollier
21 November 1908

The bust of Rémy Ollier (1816–1845), by Maurice Loumeau, was unveiled on 21 November 1908. The journalist Rémy Ollier was a pioneer for the rights of all races and liberty of the press.

Inauguration de la Statue de Sir John
Pope Hennessy
22 Décembre 1908

Inauguration of the Statue of Sir John
Pope Hennessy
22 December 1908

The statue of Sir John Pope Hennessy by Maurice Loumeau was unveiled in front of the Port Louis theatre on 22 December 1908. On 11 July 1928, this statue was relocated in front of Government House, opposite that of William Newton.

The St Sacrament procession returning to St Louis Cathedral, from the altar on the Champ de Mars, during the Feast of Corpus Christi.

From 1810 to 1968, the British colonial government maintained a military detachment on Mauritius. While they were stationed in 18th-century French military outposts, they built the future Fort Adelaide at Port Louis and erected Martello towers. After the epidemics of the 19th century, they moved into barracks in the more amenable climates of Curepipe, and later Vacoas.

Ouverture du Conseil. Maurice. 12 Avril 1938. Garde d'honneur passée en revue.

The opening of a new session of the Legislative Council on 12 April 1938. The soldiers of the British garrison could be of British, Indian or African origin. However, the officers were always British. There were many advantages in having Indian or African soldiers, such as lower pay and greater mobility.

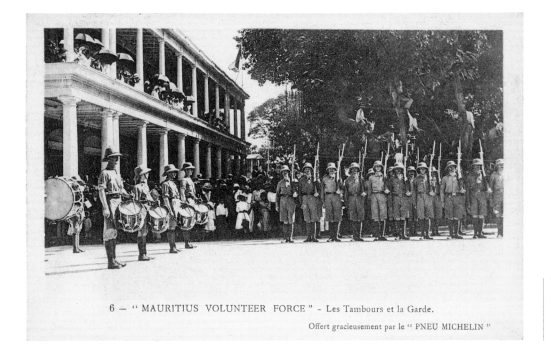

6 — " MAURITIUS VOLUNTEER FORCE " - Les Tambours et la Garde.

Offert gracieusement par le " PNEU MICHELIN "

The foreign soldiers were welcomed by the Mauritian people. Military bands were often sought after, and their performances highly appreciated. They played during official ceremonies and regularly brought balls, fun fairs and receptions to life.

The Black Watch, c 1909. This is the famous Scottish regiment, which was stationed in Mauritius at the time. Captain Hugh Rose was in command and they boasted an excellent band that played to the public in gazebos.

The „Black Watch" on Champ de Mars 1894

Cliché Gentil

259

Few Mauritians joined the British army and therefore troops were recruited from abroad.

Le „Black Watch", garde écossaise

5 — " MAURITIUS VOLUNTEER FORCE " - Le Gouverneur et les Commandants.

Offert gracieusement par le " PNEU MICHELIN "

Before being assigned to Mauritius, a regiment could have served in any country. And after Mauritius, it would be assigned elsewhere.

Offert gracieusement par le " PNEU MICHELIN "

1 — " MAURITIUS VOLUNTEER FORCE " - L'Arrivée du Gouverneur.

During the two World Wars, many Mauritians signed up to defend Britain and France. When the British military authorities did not have enough men available for the front line, the professional soldiers were called up from their posts in Mauritius. Since these soldiers then had to be replaced, it was the Mauritius Volunteer Force that maintained coastal defences.

Mauritian soldiers were sent to fight against Rommel's troops in Egypt, Libya, Tunisia, Italy and the Middle East. Others were recruited as engineers or pioneers to assist in the construction of military camps, roads and bridges.

261

Artilleurs cipayes

Upon returning to Mauritius, some of the soldiers who had fought on the front line accused those who had stayed in Mauritius of being "merely guardians of coconut trees". However, only officers could decide which soldiers were to be deployed where.

Mauritian families were fond of triumphal arches. Many families, and not just the most affluent, took advantage of any opportunity to put up an arch decorated with plants and flowers.

37 — Inauguration de la Statue du Roi Edouard VII (Port-Louis)

Edition des Magasins Réunis
Reproduction interdite

The inauguration on 24 June 1912 of the statue of King Edward VII on the Champ de Mars. It was the work of Mauritian sculptor Prosper d'Épinay, who specialized in sculpting royalty.

The Troops on the Place d'Armes
awaiting the passage of
The DUKE & DUCHESS of CORNWALL & YORK

ARRIVAL OF ROYAL BARGE

These two postcards show the arrival in Mauritius of the royal couple who were to become King George V and Queen Mary, in August 1901. The then Duke of York was the youngest son of the Prince of Wales. He ascended to the throne in 1910 and passed away in January 1936. He had just celebrated his Silver Jubilee the year before.

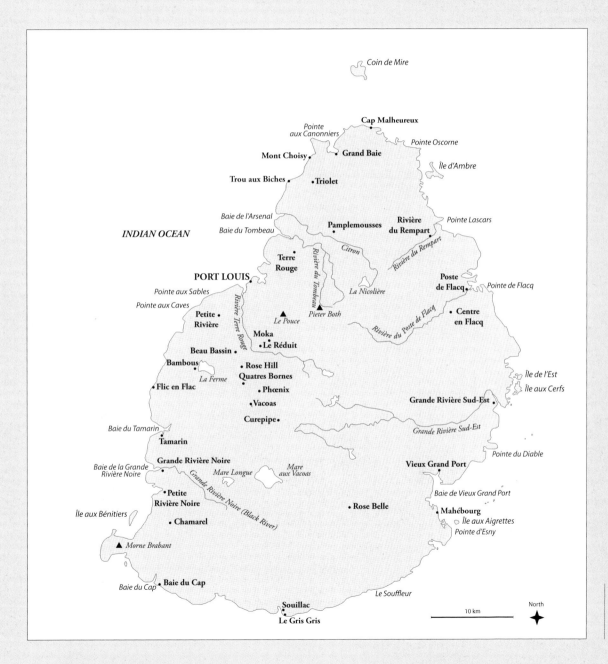

Coin de Mire

Cap Malheureux

Pointe aux Canonniers

Pointe Oscorne

•Grand Baie

Mont Choisy•

Île d'Ambre

Trou aux Biches•

•Triolet

Baie de l'Arsenal

INDIAN OCEAN

Baie du Tombeau

Pamplemousses

Rivière du Rempart

Pointe Lascars

Citron

Rivière du Rempart

Terre Rouge

Rivière du Tombeau

La Nicolière

PORT LOUIS

Pointe aux Sables

Poste de Flacq•

Pointe de Flacq

Pointe aux Caves

Petite Rivière•

Rivière Terre Rouge

▲ *Le Pouce*

▲*Pieter Both*

•Centre en Flacq

Moka•

•Le Réduit

Beau Bassin•

Rivière du Poste de Flacq

Bambous•

La Ferme

•Rose Hill

Quatres Bornes

Île de l'Est

Île aux Cerfs

•Flic en Flac

•Phœnix

•Vacoas

Grande Rivière Sud-Est

Curepipe•

Baie du Tamarin

•Tamarin

Grande Rivière Sud-Est

Grande Rivière Noire

Mare Longue

Mare aux Vacoas

Vieux Grand Port

Pointe du Diable

Baie de la Grande Rivière Noire

Grande Rivière Noire (Black River)

Baie de Vieux Grand Port

•Petite Rivière Noire

Rose Belle•

•Mahébourg

Île aux Aigrettes

Île aux Bénitiers

•Chamarel

Pointe d'Esny

▲ *Morne Brabant*

•Baie du Cap

Baie du Cap

Le Souffleur

10 km

North

Souillac

Le Gris Gris

OPPOSITE: 1782 map of Île de France by French royal cartographer Rigobert Bonne.

LEFT: Map of Mauritius, showing some key locations mentioned in this book.

ACKNOWLEDGEMENTS

This book could not have been written without the information we found in these invaluable books on the history of Mauritius: Auguste Toussaint, *Port-Louis, deux siècles d'histoire* (Port Louis: La Typographie Moderne, 1936); Antoine Chelin, *Une île et son passé* (Réunion: Bibliothèque indianocéanienne, C.R.I., Sainte-Clotilde, 1989); Guy Rouillard, *Histoire des domaines sucriers de l'île Maurice* (Mauritius: General Printing & Stationery Co. Ltd, 1964–1979); Joseph Guého and Guy Rouillard, *Les Plantes et leur histoire à l'île Maurice* (Mauritius: M.S.M. Ltd, 2000); Historical Society of Mauritius, *Dictionnaire de biographie mauricienne*, 60 booklets published from 1940 to 2011. We must not forget to add to this list the most invaluable of all – the historical work of Bishop Amédée Nagapen and Lilian Berthelot – the collection of *La Gazette des îles de la mer des Indes* (52 issues published from 1986 to 2004), and the historical and journalistic database of *Répertoire de la presse mauricienne*.

This historical information has enabled us to better appreciate the selection generously provided by André de Kervern. As a picture is worth a thousand words, we have to agree that the thousand and one details shown in each of the postcards in this album offer the best available historical picture of Mauritius before World War II. We owe an immense debt of gratitude to André de Kervern.

Our thanks also go to Didier Millet and his colleagues in Paris and Singapore. Indeed, what worth is the most beautiful postcard collection, if it cannot be shared with others?

This book is a wonderful example of democratizing the access to a source of knowledge about Mauritius, which, though relating to the past, plants deep roots for the future of our children and beyond.

Fans of *Paul et Virginie*, *Georges*, the *Dame créole*, of the Savanne in bloom, of "l'étoile et la clef de la mer des Indes", thank you.

YVAN MARTIAL

I would also like to thank Marie Claude and Didier Millet, and EDM's staff, for the great work they have achieved with my collection of antique postcards.

ANDRÉ DE KERVERN